everyday
greek

Parragon

Bath · New York · Singapore · Hong Kong · Cologne · Delhi · Melbourne

This edition published by Parragon in 2008

Parragon
Queen Street House
4 Queen Street
Bath BA1 1HE, UK

ISBN 978-1-4075-2799-4

Printed in China

This book uses both metric and imperial measurements. Follow the same units of measurement throughout; do not mix metric and imperial. All spoon measurements are level: teaspoons are assumed to be 5ml, and tablespoons are assumed to be 15ml. Unless otherwise stated, milk is assumed to be full fat, eggs and individual vegetables are medium, and pepper is freshly ground black pepper.

The times given are an approximate guide only. Optional ingredients, variations or serving suggestions have not been included in the calculations.

Recipes using raw or very lightly cooked eggs should be avoided by infants, the elderly, pregnant women, convalescents and anyone suffering from an illness. Pregnant and breastfeeding women are advised to avoid eating peanuts and peanut products. Sufferers from nut allergies should be aware that some of the ready-made ingredients used in the recipes in this book may contain nuts. Always check the packaging before use.

Vegetarians should be aware that some of the ready-made ingredients used in the recipes in this book may contain animal products. Always check the packaging before use.

everyday
greek

introduction

The cuisine of Greece is a reflection of this wonderful country of sapphire skies and turquoise seas, pretty whitewashed houses, terraced olive groves with their curiously twisted trees and, above all, of warm, generous, hospitable people. The country's culinary tradition is as long as its history and much of the food that is eaten today, especially on the smaller, unspoilt islands where a simple lifestyle is still followed, probably does not differ greatly from that enjoyed by the ancient Greeks around 2,500 years ago.

A Greek meal is a leisurely, sociable affair, often taken in the open air. The diet is based on a predominance of vegetables and salads, grilled fresh fish and meat, fruit and yogurt, all flavoured and seasoned with olive oil, lemons, wine and fragrant herbs such as thyme and oregano, which grow wild on the hillsides and are used in abundance.

A typical meal starts with a mezze, followed by a main course served with salad and crusty, freshly baked bread. Vegetables are usually served after the main course rather than with it and the meal ends with fresh fruit, a dessert or ice cream.

The emphasis is very much on the use of fresh, seasonal produce. Seafood is caught and brought in to the markets daily, sheep and goats are reared to provide meat and milk, pigs are also bred for their meat and chickens are kept for both meat and eggs. A range of vegetables – aubergines, courgettes, peppers, onions, garlic and tomatoes – is locally grown and found in every Greek kitchen, together with a few staples such as cheese, honey, canned

tuna and sardines, salted capers, olives and of course olive oil.

Greek ingredients are now readily available in other countries, so if you are an epicure – the Greek word for a lover of good food – get cooking today!

Good health!

mezzes &
soups

The Greek 'mezze' is a wonderful reflection of the country and its way of life – an irresistible collection of dips, deep-fried seafood, stuffed vine leaves, pastries, tiny sausages, olives and nuts, pleasing both to the eye and to the tastebuds, to be consumed at a relaxed and leisurely pace. If the mezze can be enjoyed out in the open air beneath a cloudless blue sky, the scene will be set to perfection.

Greek dips have become famous far beyond the boundaries of the country, perhaps the most familiar being the Smoked Cod Roe Dip, *taramasalata*, the Chickpea and Sesame Dip, *hummus* and the garlicky Cucumber and Yogurt Dip, *tzatziki*, which also works as a delicious chilled soup with the addition of chicken stock. Soups are popular in Greece, particularly the classic *soúpa avgolémono*, a simple consommé thickened and flavoured with an egg and lemon sauce and the filling and satisfying Fishermen's Soup, traditionally made with the catch of the day.

The mezze is always served with bread, often the soft, flat pitta bread that is ideal for scooping up dips or stuffing with sausages and salad, and accompanied by a glass of beer, wine or the distinctive aniseed-flavoured apéritif, ouzo, which you either hate – or absolutely love!

smoked cod roe dip

ingredients

SERVES 6

225 g/8 oz smoked cod roe or
    fresh grey mullet roe
1 small onion, quartered
55 g/2 oz fresh white
    breadcrumbs
1 large garlic clove, crushed
grated rind and juice of
    1 large lemon
150 ml/5 fl oz extra-virgin
    olive oil
6 tbsp hot water
pepper
black Greek olives, capers
    and chopped flat-leaf
    parsley, to garnish
warm pitta bread or potato
    crisps, to serve

method

1 Remove the skin from the fish roe. Put the onion in a food processor and chop finely. Add the cod roe in small pieces and blend until smooth. Add the breadcrumbs, garlic, lemon rind and juice and mix well together.

2 With the machine running, very slowly pour in the oil. When all the oil has been incorporated, blend in the water. Season with pepper.

3 Pour the mixture into a serving bowl and chill in the refrigerator for at least 1 hour before serving.

4 Serve garnished with olives, capers and chopped parsley and accompany with warm pitta bread or crisps.

smoked red pepper dip

ingredients

SERVES 6

4 large smoked red peppers
    and juice from the jar
100 g/3½ oz full-fat
    cream cheese
½ tsp lemon juice
salt and pepper
warm pitta bread, to serve

method

1 Chop the peppers very finely and put in a bowl. Add the cheese, 1 tablespoon of juice from the jar of peppers, the lemon juice, salt and pepper and stir gently until mixed.

2 Chill in the refrigerator for at least 1 hour before serving.

3 To serve, stir the mixture and transfer to a serving bowl. Accompany with warm pitta bread.

chickpea & sesame dip

ingredients

SERVES 8

225 g/8 oz dried chickpeas,
    covered with water and
    soaked overnight
juice of 2 large lemons
150 ml/5 fl oz tahini paste
2 garlic cloves, crushed
4 tbsp extra-virgin olive oil
small pinch of ground cumin
salt and pepper
1 tsp paprika
chopped flat-leaf parsley,
    to garnish
pitta bread, to serve

method

1 Drain the chickpeas, put in a saucepan and cover with cold water. Bring to the boil then simmer for about 2 hours or until very tender.

2 Drain the chickpeas, reserving a little of the liquid, and put in a food processor, reserving a few to garnish. Blend the chickpeas until smooth, gradually adding the lemon juice and enough reserved liquid to form a smooth, thick purée.

3 Add the tahini paste, garlic, 3 tablespoons of the olive oil and the cumin and blend until smooth. Season with salt and pepper.

4 Turn the mixture into a shallow serving dish and chill in the refrigerator for 2–3 hours before serving.

5 To serve, mix the reserved olive oil with the paprika and drizzle over the top of the dish. Sprinkle with the parsley and the reserved chickpeas. Accompany with warm pitta bread.

cucumber & yogurt dip

ingredients

SERVES 4

1 small cucumber

300 ml/10 fl oz authentic
    Greek yogurt

1 large garlic clove, crushed

1 tbsp chopped fresh mint
    or dill

salt and pepper

warm pitta bread, to serve

method

1 Peel then coarsely grate the cucumber.
Put in a sieve and squeeze out as much of
the water as possible. Put the cucumber into
a bowl.

2 Add the yogurt, garlic and chopped mint
(reserve a little as a garnish, if desired) to the
cucumber, season with pepper and mix
together thoroughly.

3 Chill in the refrigerator for about 2 hours
before serving.

4 To serve, stir the cucumber and yogurt dip
and transfer to a serving bowl. Sprinkle with
salt and accompany with warmed pitta bread.

almond & garlic dip

ingredients

SERVES 6

55 g/2 oz day-old bread,
about 2 slices

250 g/9 oz almonds

4–6 large garlic cloves,
roughly chopped

150 ml/5 fl oz extra-virgin
olive oil

2 tbsp white wine vinegar

salt and pepper

fresh coriander or flat-leaf
parsley sprigs, to garnish

sesame breadsticks, to serve

method

1 Cut the crusts off the bread and tear the bread into small pieces. Put in a bowl, pour over enough water to cover and set aside to soak for 10–15 minutes. Squeeze the bread dry, then set aside.

2 To blanch the almonds, put them in a heatproof bowl and pour over just enough boiling water to cover. Stand for 30 seconds, then drain. The skins should slide off easily.

3 Transfer the almonds and garlic to a food processor and process until finely chopped. Add the squeezed bread and process again until well blended.

4 With the motor running, gradually add the olive oil through the feeder tube in a thin, steady stream until a thick paste forms. Add the vinegar and process again. Season with salt and pepper to taste.

5 Scrape the mixture into a bowl, cover and chill until required. It will keep in the refrigerator for up to 4 days. To serve, garnish with herb sprigs. Serve with sesame breadsticks.

aubergine & garlic dip

ingredients

SERVES 6

2 large aubergines
50 ml/2 fl oz extra-virgin
    olive oil
juice of 1/2 lemon
150 ml/5 fl oz authentic
    Greek yogurt
2 garlic cloves, crushed
pinch of ground cumin
salt and pepper
chopped fresh flat-leaf
    parsley, to garnish
strips of red and green
    pepper or sesame
    crackers (see page 38),
    to serve

method

1 Prick the skins of the aubergines with a fork and put on a baking sheet. Bake in a preheated oven, 190°C/375°F, for 45 minutes or until very soft. Leave to cool slightly, then cut the aubergines in half lengthways and scoop out the flesh.

2 Heat the oil in a large, heavy frying pan, add the aubergine flesh and fry for 5 minutes. Put the aubergine mixture into a food processor, add the lemon juice and blend until smooth. Gradually add the yogurt, then the garlic and cumin. Season with salt and pepper.

3 Pour the mixture into a serving bowl and chill in the refrigerator for at least 1 hour.

4 Garnish with chopped fresh parsley and serve with strips of raw pepper or sesame crackers.

split pea dip

ingredients

SERVES 6

250 g/9 oz yellow split peas

2 small onions, 1 chopped
    roughly and 1 chopped
    very finely

1 garlic clove, chopped
    roughly

6 tbsp extra-virgin olive oil

1 tbsp chopped fresh oregano

salt and pepper

savoury crackers, to serve

method

1 Rinse the split peas under cold running water. Put in a saucepan and add the roughly chopped onion, the garlic and plenty of cold water. Bring to the boil then simmer for about 45 minutes or until very tender.

2 Drain the split peas, reserving a little of the cooking liquid, and put in a food processor. Add 5 tablespoons of the olive oil and blend until smooth. If the mixture seems too dry, add enough of the reserved liquid to form a smooth, thick purée. Add the oregano and season with salt and pepper.

3 Pour the mixture into a serving bowl and sprinkle with the finely chopped onion and extra oregano if desired. Drizzle over the remaining olive oil.

4 Serve warm or cold with pitta bread.

greek garlic sauce

ingredients

SERVES 6–8

115 g/4 oz whole blanched
    almonds

3 tbsp fresh white
    breadcrumbs

2 large garlic cloves, crushed

2 tsp lemon juice

salt and pepper

150 ml/5 fl oz extra-virgin
    olive oil

4 tbsp hot water

pitta bread and raw
    vegetables such as
    peppers, cucumber and
    carrots, to serve

method

1 Put the almonds in a food processor and process until finely ground. Add the breadcrumbs, garlic, lemon juice, salt and pepper and mix together well.

2 With the machine running, very slowly pour in the oil to form a smooth, thick mixture. When all the oil has been added, blend in the water.

3 Pour the mixture into a serving bowl and chill in the refrigerator for at least 2 hours.

4 Serve with pitta bread and raw vegetables.

greek sausages

ingredients

MAKES ABOUT 24

350 g/12 oz ground pork
115 g/4 oz ground beef
1 garlic clove, crushed
$1/2$ tsp ground cinnamon
$1/4$ tsp dried savory or thyme
grated rind of 1 small orange
8 black peppercorns, crushed
100 ml/$3^1/2$ fl oz dry
    red wine
lemon wedges, to garnish

method

1 Put all the ingredients except the lemon wedges in a bowl and mix well together. Cover and marinate in the refrigerator overnight or for about 12 hours.

2 Preheat the grill. Stir the mixture and then, with damp hands, form into about 24 small sausage shapes about 5 cm/2 inches long and place on a grill pan.

3 Grill the sausages for about 15 minutes, turning several times, until brown on all sides.

4 Serve hot, garnished with lemon wedges.

deep-fried squid

ingredients

SERVES 6

900 g/2 lb small cleaned
    squid
115 g/4 oz plain flour
salt and pepper
sunflower oil, for deep-frying

method

1 Rinse and dry the squid. Slice the bodies into rings, leaving the tentacles whole. Season the flour with salt and pepper. Dip the pieces of squid in the flour, making sure they are well coated, then shake off any excess.

2 Heat the oil in a deep-fat fryer to 180°C/ 350°F, or when a cube of bread, dropped into the fat, turns brown in 1 minute. When the oil is hot, add the squid in small batches and fry for about 1 minute or until crisp and golden. Remove from the fryer with a slotted spoon and drain on kitchen paper. Continue to cook the remaining squid in small batches.

3 Sprinkle lightly with salt and serve hot.

stuffed vine leaves

ingredients

MAKES ABOUT 30

225-g/8-oz pack vine leaves
    preserved in brine
115 g/4 oz risotto or other
    short-grain rice
175 ml/6 fl oz olive oil
1 small onion, chopped finely
1 garlic clove, chopped finely
55 g/2 oz pine nuts, chopped
55 g/2 oz currants
3 spring onions, chopped
    finely
1 tbsp chopped fresh mint
1 tbsp chopped fresh dill
2 tbsp chopped fresh flat-leaf
    parsley
salt and pepper
juice of 1 lemon
lemon wedges and authentic
    Greek yogurt, to serve

method

1 Place the vine leaves in a bowl, add boiling water and soak for 20 minutes. Drain, soak in cold water for 20 minutes and drain again.

2 Meanwhile, cover the rice with cold water in a saucepan, bring to the boil, then simmer for 15–20 minutes or until tender. Drain well and set aside in a bowl to cool.

3 Heat 2 tablespoons of the oil in a frying pan and fry the onion and garlic until softened. Add to the rice with the pine nuts, currants, spring onions, mint, dill and parsley. Season with a little salt and plenty of pepper and mix well.

4 Place one vine leaf, vein-side upward, on a work surface. Put a little filling on the base of the leaf and fold up the bottom end of the leaf. Fold in the sides, then roll up the leaf around the filling. Squeeze gently to seal. Fill and roll the remaining leaves, then pack the stuffed leaves close together in a large flameproof casserole, seam-side down and in a single layer.

5 Mix the remaining oil and the lemon juice with 150 ml/5 fl oz water and pour into the casserole. Place a large plate over the vine leaves to keep them in place then cover the casserole with a lid. Bring to simmering point then simmer for 45 minutes. Leave the vine leaves to cool in the liquid.

6 Serve warm or chilled, with lemon wedges and yogurt.

greek beans

ingredients

SERVES 4

400 g/14 oz canned
cannellini beans, drained
and rinsed

1 tbsp olive oil

3 garlic cloves, crushed

425 ml/15 fl oz vegetable
stock

1 bay leaf

2 fresh oregano sprigs

1 tbsp tomato purée

juice of 1 lemon

1 small red onion, chopped

25 g/1 oz pitted black Greek
olives, halved

salt and pepper

method

1 Put the beans in an ovenproof casserole over low heat, add the oil and garlic and cook, stirring frequently, for 4–5 minutes.

2 Add the stock, bay leaf, oregano, tomato purée, lemon juice and onion and stir well to mix. Cover and simmer for 1 hour or until the sauce has thickened.

3 Stir in the olives, then season to taste with salt and pepper.

4 This dish is delicious served either warm or cold.

hot roasted nuts

ingredients

MAKES 8 OZ/225 G

2 tbsp olive oil

225 g/8 oz shelled pistachio
     nuts, almonds or
     walnut halves

3 tbsp chopped fresh sage,
     thyme, marjoram or
     oregano

1 tsp paprika or cumin

salt

method

1 Put the oil in a roasting tin and swirl around
to cover the bottom. Add the nuts and toss to
coat evenly in the oil, then spread out in a
single layer. Sprinkle with the herbs, paprika
or cumin and salt.

2 Bake in a preheated oven, 170°C/325°F, for
20 minutes, tossing the nuts occasionally as
they cook.

3 Drain, if necessary, on kitchen paper and
serve warm.

olive bread

ingredients

MAKES 2 MEDIUM LOAVES

900 g/2 lbs strong white
    bread flour

1 packet easy-blend
    dried yeast

3 tsp sesame seeds

1 tsp salt

1/2 tsp dried oregano

3 tbsp olive oil, plus extra
    for brushing

600 ml/1 pint warm water

225 g/8 oz Greek olives,
    pitted and chopped
    roughly

method

1 Put the flour, yeast, 2 teaspoons of the sesame seeds, the salt and oregano in a large bowl and mix. Add 3 tablespoons of the olive oil and, using a wooden spoon, gradually add the water to form a firm dough.

2 Turn the dough onto a lightly floured work surface and knead for 10 minutes or until smooth. Put the dough in a clean bowl, cover with a clean, damp tea towel and set to rise in a warm place for about 1 hour or until doubled in size.

3 Turn the dough onto a lightly floured work surface and knead lightly to knock out the air, then knead in the olives. Divide the dough into 2 pieces and shape each piece into a smooth round. Place on a lightly oiled baking sheet, cover with a clean tea towel and set in a warm place for about 30 minutes or until doubled in size.

4 Using a sharp knife, make slashes across the top of each loaf then lightly brush with olive oil and sprinkle the remaining sesame seeds on top.

5 Bake in a preheated oven, 220°C/425°F, for 10 minutes, then reduce the temperature to 190°C/375°F and bake for another 25 minutes or until risen and brown and the bread sounds hollow when tapped on the bottom. Cool on a wire rack.

walnut cheese wafers

ingredients

MAKES ABOUT 38

40 g/1 1/2 oz walnut pieces

115 g/4 oz plus 1 tbsp plain
   flour

salt and pepper

115 g/4 oz butter

115 g/4 oz authentic Greek
   feta cheese

beaten egg, for glazing

method

1 Put the walnuts in a food processor and chop finely. Remove from the processor and set aside.

2 Add the flour, salt and pepper to the processor bowl. Cut the butter into small pieces, add to the flour and mix in short bursts, until the mixture resembles fine breadcrumbs. Coarsely grate in the cheese, add the reserved walnuts and mix quickly to form a dough.

3 Turn the mixture onto a lightly floured work surface and roll out thinly. Using a 6-cm/ 2 1/4-inch round biscuit cutter, cut the dough into rounds and place on baking sheets. Brush the tops with beaten egg.

4 Bake the wafers in a preheated oven, 190°C/375°F, for about 10 minutes or until golden. Cool on a wire rack.

5 Store in an airtight tin.

sesame crackers

ingredients

MAKES ABOUT 30

150 g/5^1/$_2$ oz plain flour, plus
    extra for dusting
3 tbsp sesame seeds
finely grated rind of 1 lemon
2 tbsp chopped fresh thyme
^{1}/$_2$ tsp salt
freshly ground pepper
2 tbsp butter
3–4 tbsp cold water
1 small egg white

method

1 Put the flour, 2 tablespoons of the sesame seeds, the lemon rind, thyme, salt and pepper in a bowl. Cut the butter into small pieces and rub into the mixture until it resembles fine breadcrumbs. Gradually stir in the water until the mixture forms a firm dough.

2 Turn the mixture onto a lightly floured work surface and roll out thinly. Using a 5-cm/2-inch round biscuit cutter, cut the dough into rounds and place on baking sheets.

3 Brush the crackers with the egg white and sprinkle with the remaining sesame seeds. Bake in in a preheated oven, 190°C/375°F, for 20–25 minutes or until lightly browned. Cool on a wire rack.

4 Store the crackers in an airtight tin.

greek feta & olive tartlets

ingredients

MAKES 12

butter, for greasing

plain flour, for dusting

175 g/6 oz pastry

1 egg

3 egg yolks

300 ml/10 fl oz whipping
    cream

salt and pepper

115 g/4 oz authentic Greek
    feta cheese

6 pitted black Greek
    olives, halved

12 small fresh rosemary sprigs

method

1 Grease 12 individual 6-cm/2^1/2-inch tart
tins, or the cups in a 12-hole muffin pan.

2 On a floured work surface, roll out the pastry
to 3 mm/^{1}/8 inch thick. Cut the pastry into
rounds, use to line the prepared tins and prick
the bottoms with a fork. Press a square of foil
into each tartlet casel and bake in the preheated
oven for 12 minutes. Remove the foil and bake
for a further 3 minutes.

3 Place the egg, egg yolks and cream in a
bowl, add salt and pepper to taste and beat
together.

4 Crumble the feta cheese into the tartlet
cases and spoon over the egg mixture. Place
half an olive and a rosemary sprig on top of
each tartlet, then bake in a preheated oven,
200°C/400°F, for 15 minutes or until the filling
is just set.

5 Serve warm or cold.

hot cheese pastries

ingredients

MAKES ABOUT 32

200 g/7 oz authentic Greek
feta cheese

115 g/4 oz cottage cheese

3 tbsp chopped fresh flat-leaf
parsley

2 eggs, beaten

pepper

8 sheets authentic Greek filo
pastry (work with one
sheet at a time and keep
the remaining sheets
covered with a damp
tea towel)

100 ml/3½ fl oz olive oil

method

1 Crumble the feta cheese into a bowl. Add
the cottage cheese, parsley and eggs and beat
with a fork until well blended. Season with
pepper.

2 Cut the filo pastry lengthways into 7-cm/2³/4-
inch strips. Take one strip and brush it with
olive oil. Put a heaped teaspoon of the cheese
mixture on the bottom left-hand corner. Fold
over the corner with the filling so that it meets
the long side edge and forms a triangle.
Continue folding the filling up and over from
side to side to form a neat triangle. Place the
pastry on an oiled baking sheet and brush
with oil. Continue until all the pastry strips and
the filling have been used.

3 Bake the pastries in a preheated oven,
190°C/375°F, for about 15 minutes until
golden brown. Serve hot.

consommé with egg & lemon sauce

ingredients

SERVES 4–6

1.4 litres/2½ pints chicken stock

55 g/2 oz risotto or other short-grain rice

2 eggs

6 tbsp fresh lemon juice

salt and pepper

thin lemon slices, to garnish

finely chopped fresh flat-leaf parsley, to garnish

method

1 Pour the stock into a large saucepan and bring to the boil. Add the rice, return to the boil, then simmer for 15–20 minutes, or according to the instructions on the packet, until tender.

2 Meanwhile, put the eggs and lemon juice in a bowl and whisk together until frothy.

3 When the rice is cooked, lower the heat and, whisking all the time, gradually add a ladleful of the stock to the lemon mixture. Pour the mixture into the soup and simmer, still whisking, until the soup thickens slightly. (Do not boil the mixture or it will curdle.) Season to taste with salt and pepper.

4 Ladle the soup into individual serving bowls and garnish with lemon slices and chopped parsley. Serve hot.

fishermen's soup

ingredients

SERVES 6

900 g/2 lb fillets of mixed
    white fish and shellfish,
    such as cod, flounder,
    halibut, monkfish, sea
    bass, whiting and
    peeled prawns
150 ml/5 fl oz olive oil
2 large onions, sliced
2 celery stalks, sliced thinly
2 garlic cloves, chopped
150 ml/5 fl oz white wine
4 canned tomatoes, chopped
pared rind of 1 orange
1 tsp chopped fresh thyme
2 tbsp chopped fresh parsley
2 bay leaves
salt and pepper
lemon wedges, to serve
croûtons, to garnish

method

1 Cut the fish into fairly large, thick serving portions, discarding any skin. Heat the oil in a large saucepan, add the onion, celery and garlic and fry for 5 minutes or until softened.

2 Add the fish and prawns to the pan, then add the wine, tomatoes, pared orange rind, thyme, parsley, bay leaves, salt, pepper and enough cold water to cover. Bring to the boil, then simmer, uncovered, for 15 minutes.

3 Serve the soup hot, with lemon wedges and garnished with croûtons.

bean & vegetable soup

ingredients

SERVES 4

225 g/8 oz dried haricot or
   cannellini beans, covered
   with water and soaked
   overnight
850 ml/1^1/$_2$ pints water
2 onions, chopped coarsely
2 garlic cloves, chopped
2 carrots, chopped coarsely
2 celery stalks, sliced thinly
3 tbsp olive oil
2 tsp chopped fresh thyme
1 bay leaf
pinch of sugar
400 g/14 oz canned tomatoes
   in juice
salt and pepper
55 g/2 oz black Greek olives,
   pitted and chopped
2 tbsp chopped fresh flat-leaf
   parsley

method

1 Drain the soaked beans, rinse under cold water, then put in a large saucepan. Add the water, bring to the boil and boil for 10 minutes. Reduce the heat, cover the pan and simmer for 30 minutes.

2 Add the onions, garlic, carrots, celery, oil, thyme, bay leaf, sugar and the tomatoes with their juice, breaking them up with a fork. Season with pepper. (Do not add salt at this stage because it will make the beans tough.)

3 Return to simmering point, cover the pan again and simmer for 45 minutes to 1 hour or until the beans are tender.

4 Season the soup with salt and pepper and serve hot, sprinkled with the chopped olives and the parsley.

roasted vegetable soup

ingredients

SERVES 6

2 aubergines

4 tomatoes

2 red peppers

2 onions, unpeeled

2 garlic cloves, unpeeled

4 tbsp olive oil

sprig of fresh oregano

salt and pepper

1½ litres/2¾ pints chicken
    or vegetable stock

fresh basil leaves or chopped
    fresh parsley, to garnish

method

1 Prick the aubergine skins with a fork and put in a roasting tin. Add the tomatoes, peppers, unpeeled onions and garlic. Sprinkle with 2 tablespoons of the olive oil. Roast in a preheated oven, 180°C/350°F, for 30 minutes, then remove the tomatoes. Roast the remaining vegetables for a further 30 minutes or until soft and the pepper skins have blackened.

2 Put the cooked roasted vegetables in a bowl, cover with a damp tea towel and leave until cold. When cold, cut the aubergines in half, scoop out the flesh and put in another bowl. Remove the skin from the tomatoes, cut in half, discard the seeds and add the flesh to the bowl. Hold the peppers over the bowl to collect the juices and peel off the skin. Remove the stem, core and seeds and add the flesh to the bowl. Peel the onions, cut into quarters and add to the bowl. Squeeze the garlic cloves out of their skins into the bowl.

3 Heat the remaining olive oil in a large saucepan, add the vegetables and their juices, the leaves from the oregano, salt and pepper and cook gently for about 30 minutes, stirring frequently. Add the stock to the pan, bring to the boil, then simmer for 30 minutes.

4 Allow the soup to cool slightly, then purée in a food processor or blender. If necessary, reheat the soup. Serve hot, garnished with basil leaves or chopped parsley.

fresh herb soup

ingredients

SERVES 4

large bunch fresh coriander

600 ml/1 pint chicken or
    vegetable stock

1 small onion, chopped
    roughly

1 large garlic clove, chopped
    finely

finely grated rind and juice of
    1 small lemon

salt and pepper

300 ml/10 fl oz authentic
    Greek yogurt

method

1 Remove the leaves from the coriander, reserving the stems, finely chop and set aside. Roughly chop the stems. Put the stems, stock, onion, garlic, lemon rind, salt and pepper in a saucepan and simmer for 30 minutes.

2 Strain the stock and return to the rinsed pan. Add the lemon juice and yogurt and simmer for 2–3 minutes or until hot. (Do not boil or the soup will curdle.)

3 Add the reserved chopped coriander and serve hot.

yogurt & tomato soup

ingredients

SERVES 4

4 large tomatoes

2 tbsp olive oil

1 onion, chopped roughly

1 garlic clove, chopped

300 ml/10 fl oz vegetable
    stock

2 oil-packed sun-dried
    tomatoes, chopped

1 tsp chopped fresh thyme

$^1/_2$ tsp ground cinnamon

salt and pepper

300 ml/10 fl oz authentic
    Greek yogurt

method

1 Coarsely grate the tomatoes into a bowl, discarding their skins left in your hand. Heat the oil in a saucepan, add the onion and garlic and fry for 5 minutes or until softened. Add the tomatoes to the pan and cook gently for a further 5 minutes.

2 Add the stock, sun-dried tomatoes, thyme, cinnamon, salt and pepper, bring to the boil, then simmer for 10 minutes.

3 Allow the soup to cool slightly then purée in a food processor or blender, or with a handheld blender. Add the yogurt and mix. Adjust the seasoning if necessary.

4 If serving hot, reheat the soup gently. (Do not boil or the soup will curdle.) If serving cold, cool and then chill in the refrigerator for 3–4 hours.

chilled cucumber soup

ingredients

SERVES 4

2 medium cucumbers

300 ml/10 fl oz authentic
    Greek yogurt

300 ml/10 fl oz chicken stock

2 tbsp walnut oil

1 large garlic clove, crushed

3 tbsp chopped fresh dill

salt and pepper

115 g/4 oz walnut pieces,
    chopped

method

1 Peel the cucumbers and chop the flesh into small dice. Beat the yogurt with the chicken stock, the walnut oil, garlic and dill, reserving a little dill to garnish. Stir in the chopped cucumber and season with salt and pepper.

2 Chill the soup in the refrigerator for at least 4 hours.

3 Stir in the chopped walnuts and serve garnished with the reserved chopped dill.

meat &
poultry

The Greek countryside is not ideal for grazing and for this reason meat is expensive and reserved for festive occasions, of which there are many, as most Greeks observe the saints' days. Making a little go a long way has its advantages, however – some of the most appetizing, best-known and best-loved classic Greek meat-based dishes, such as the aubergine-layered *moussaka* and the Baked Pasta with Spicy Meat Sauce, *pastitsio*, have evolved as a means of making a robust, satisfying dish with only a small amount of meat. Caltle are the most difficult animals to rear successfully and are often slaughtered young to produce veal. Pigs are more easily reared, but it is sheep and goats that take most readily to the lightly grassed hillsides and lamb, followed by kid, is the most prevalent and popular meat in Greek cuisine.

Chickens were traditionally kept by all Greek families and are still to be seen wandering about in mainland villages and on the islands. They are also bred commercially now and because they are usually free-range and corn-fed, they have an excellent flavour. Chickens are most often served roasted, but Chicken Kebabs with Yogurt Sauce is a favourite Greek dish, not to be missed.

moussaka

ingredients

SERVES 4

2 aubergines, thinly sliced

450 g/1 lb fresh lean minced
    beef or lamb

2 onions, thinly sliced

1 tsp finely chopped garlic

400 g/14 oz canned tomatoes

2 tbsp chopped fresh parsley

salt and pepper

2 eggs

300 ml/10 fl oz low-fat natural
    yogurt

1 tbsp freshly grated
    Parmesan cheese

method

1 Dry-fry the aubergine slices, in batches, in a non-stick frying pan on both sides until browned. Remove from the pan.

2 Add the beef or lamb to the frying pan and cook for 5 minutes, stirring, until browned. Stir in the onions and garlic and cook for a further 5 minutes or until browned. Add the tomatoes, parsley, salt and pepper, then bring to the boil and simmer for 20 minutes or until the meat is tender.

3 Arrange half the aubergine slices in a layer in an ovenproof dish. Add the meat mixture, then the remaining aubergine slices.

4 Beat the eggs in a bowl, then beat in the yogurt and add salt and pepper to taste. Pour the mixture over the aubergines and sprinkle the grated cheese on top.

5 Bake the moussaka in a preheated oven, 180°C/350°F, for 45 minutes or until golden brown. Serve straight from the dish.

grecian meatballs

ingredients

SERVES 4

450 g/1 lb lean, finely minced
 beef or lamb

1 medium onion

1 garlic clove, crushed

25 g/1 oz fresh white or
 brown breadcrumbs

1 tbsp chopped fresh mint

1 tbsp chopped fresh parsley

salt and pepper

1 egg, beaten

olive oil, for brushing

rice or warm pitta bread,
 to serve

method

1 Put the minced beef or lamb in a bowl. Grate in the onion, then add the garlic, breadcrumbs, mint and parsley. Season well with salt and pepper. Mix the ingredients well then add the beaten egg and mix to bind the mixture together.

2 With damp hands, form the mixture into 16 small balls and thread onto 4 flat metal skewers. Lightly oil a grill pan and brush the meatballs with oil.

3 Preheat the grill and cook the meatballs under a medium heat for 10 minutes, turning frequently and brushing with more oil if necessary, until browned. Serve the meatballs with rice or tucked into warm pitta bread.

thick beef & baby onion casserole

ingredients

SERVES 6

2 tbsp olive oil

450 g/1 lb baby onions, peeled and left whole

2 garlic cloves, peeled and halved

900 g/2 lb stewing beef, cubed

$^1/_2$ tsp ground cinnamon

1 tsp ground cloves

1 tsp ground cumin

2 tbsp tomato purée

salt and pepper

1 bottle full-bodied red wine

grated rind and juice of 1 orange

1 bay leaf

chopped fresh flat-leaf parsley, to garnish

boiled or mashed potatoes, to serve

method

1 Heat the oil in a large flameproof casserole. Add the whole onions and the garlic and fry for 5 minutes or until softened and beginning to brown. Add the beef to the casserole and fry for about 5 minutes, stirring frequently, until browned on all sides.

2 Stir the cinnamon, cloves, cumin, tomato purée, salt and pepper into the casserole. Pour in the wine, stirring in any glazed bits from the bottom, then add the grated orange rind and juice and the bay leaf. Bring to the boil, then cover the casserole.

3 Cook in a preheated oven, 150°C/300°F, for about 1$^1/4$ hours. Remove the lid and cook the casserole for another hour, stirring once or twice during this time, until the meat is tender.

4 Garnish with chopped fresh parsley and serve hot, with boiled or mashed potatoes.

braised veal in red wine

ingredients

SERVES 6

4 tbsp plain flour

salt and pepper

900 g/2 lb stewing veal or
    beef, cubed

4 tbsp olive oil

350 g/12 oz pickling onions,
    peeled and left whole

2 garlic cloves, chopped
    finely

350 g/12 oz sliced carrots

300 ml/10 fl oz dry red wine

150 ml/5 fl oz beef or chicken
    stock

400 g/14 oz canned chopped
    tomatoes with herbs in juice

pared rind of 1 lemon

1 bay leaf

1 tbsp chopped fresh flat-leaf
    parsley

1 tbsp chopped fresh basil

1 tsp chopped fresh thyme

rice, to serve

method

1 Put the flour and pepper in a plastic bag, add the meat and shake well to coat each piece. Heat the oil in a large flameproof casserole. Add the meat and fry, in batches, for 5–10 minutes, stirring constantly, until browned on all sides. Remove with a slotted spoon and set aside.

2 Add the whole onions, garlic and carrots to the casserole and fry for 5 minutes or until beginning to soften. Return the meat to the casserole.

3 Pour in the wine, stirring in any glazed bits from the bottom, then add the stock, the tomatoes with their juice, lemon rind, bay leaf, parsley, basil, thyme, salt and pepper. Bring to the boil, then cover the casserole.

4 Cook in a preheated oven, 180°C/350°F, for about 2 hours or until the meat is tender.

5 Serve hot with rice.

baked pasta with spicy meat sauce

ingredients

SERVES 4–6

2 tbsp olive oil

1 onion, chopped finely

2 garlic cloves, chopped finely

650 g/1 lb 7 oz lean minced
    lamb or beef

400 g/14 oz canned chopped
    tomatoes in juice

pinch of sugar

2 tbsp chopped fresh flat-leaf
    parsley

1 tbsp chopped fresh
    marjoram

1 tsp ground cinnamon

1/2 tsp grated nutmeg

1/4 tsp ground cloves

salt and pepper

225 g/8 oz long, hollow
    Greek macaroni or other
    short pasta

2 eggs, beaten

300 ml/10 fl oz authentic
    Greek yogurt

55 g/2 oz authentic Greek
    feta cheese, grated

25 g/1 oz kefalotiri or
    pecorino cheese, grated

method

1 Heat the oil in a saucepan, add the onion and garlic and fry for 5 minutes or until softened. Add the lamb or beef to the pan and fry for about 5 minutes or until browned all over, stirring frequently and breaking up the meat.

2 Add the tomatoes, sugar, parsley, marjoram, cinnamon, nutmeg, cloves, salt and pepper. Bring to the boil, then simmer, uncovered, for 30 minutes, stirring occasionally.

3 Meanwhile, cook the macaroni in a large saucepan of boiling salted water for 10–12 minutes or as directed on the packet, until tender, then drain well.

4 Beat together the eggs, yogurt and feta cheese. Season with salt and pepper.

5 When the meat is cooked, transfer it to a large ovenproof dish. Add the macaroni in a layer to cover the meat then pour over the sauce. Sprinkle over the kefalotiri or pecorino cheese.

6 Bake in a preheated oven, 190°C/375°F, for 30–45 minutes or until golden brown. Serve hot or warm, cut into portions.

aubergine cake

ingredients

SERVES 6

6 tbsp olive oil

1 large onion, sliced

2 celery stalks, sliced thinly

450 g/1 lb minced lamb

3 tbsp tomato purée

150 g/5$^{1}/_{2}$ oz bottled sun-
   dried tomatoes, drained
   and chopped

1 tsp dried oregano

1 tbsp red wine vinegar

150 ml/5 fl oz chicken stock

salt and pepper

1 aubergine, sliced thinly

6 tbsp butter

40 g/1$^{1}/_{2}$ oz plain flour

600 ml/1 pint milk

200 g/7 oz kefalotiri or
   pecorino cheese, grated

225 g/8 oz dried fusilli

1 tbsp butter for greasing

method

1 Heat 2 tablespoons of the olive oil in a saucepan over low heat. Add the onion and celery and cook for 3–4 minutes. Add the lamb and cook, stirring frequently, until browned. Stir in the tomato purée, sun-dried tomatoes, oregano, red wine vinegar and chicken stock and season to taste. Bring to the boil and cook for 20 minutes.

2 Heat the remaining oil in a frying pan over medium heat. Add the aubergine slices in batches and cook for 4 minutes on each side. Remove and drain.

3 Put the butter, flour and milk in a saucepan and heat gently, whisking vigorously with a balloon whisk, until the sauce thickens, boils and is smooth. Simmer for 1–2 minutes. Remove from the heat. Stir in 140 g/5 oz of the kefalotiri or pecorino cheese.

4 Bring a large saucepan of lightly salted water to the boil over medium heat. Add the pasta and cook until almost done. Drain thoroughly, then stir in half of the cheese sauce.

5 Layer the pasta, lamb sauce and aubergine slices in a greased dish. Spread the remaining cheese sauce over the top, then sprinkle with the remaining cheese. Cook in a preheated oven, 190°C/375°F, for 25 minutes. Serve hot or warm.

roast lamb with orzo

ingredients

SERVES 4

750 g/1 lb 10 oz boned leg or
    shoulder of lamb

¹/₂ lemon, sliced thinly

1 tbsp chopped fresh oregano

4 large garlic cloves, 2 chopped
    finely and 2 sliced thinly

salt and pepper

800 g/1 lb 12 oz canned
    chopped tomatoes in juice

pinch of sugar

1 bay leaf

2 tbsp olive oil

250 g/9 oz orzo or short
    grain rice

method

1 If necessary, untie the leg of lamb and open out. Place the lemon slices down the middle, sprinkle over half the oregano, the chopped garlic and salt and pepper to taste. Roll up the meat and tie with string. Using the tip of a sharp knife, make slits in the lamb and insert the garlic slices.

2 Calculate the cooking time, allowing 25 minutes per pound plus 25 minutes.

3 Put the tomatoes and their juice, 150 ml/ 5 fl oz cold water, the remaining oregano, sugar and bay leaf in a large roasting tin. Place the lamb on top, drizzle over the olive oil and season with salt and pepper.

4 Roast the lamb in a preheated oven, 180°C/350°F, for the calculated cooking time. Fifteen minutes before the lamb is cooked, stir 150 ml/5 fl oz boiling water and the orzo into the tomatoes. Add a little extra water if the sauce seems too thick. Return to the oven for another 15 minutes or until the lamb and orzo are tender and the tomatoes are reduced to a thick sauce.

5 To serve, carve the lamb into slices and serve hot with the orzo and tomato sauce.

lamb & aubergine moussaka

ingredients

SERVES 6–8

2 tbsp olive oil, plus extra for
    shallow-frying

1 large onion, chopped
    roughly

1 large garlic clove, chopped
    finely

1 kg/2 lb 4 oz lean
    minced lamb

100 ml/3$^{1}/_{2}$ fl oz dry
    red wine

2 tbsp tomato purée

sugar

$^{1}/_{4}$ tsp ground cinnamon

1 tbsp chopped fresh oregano
    or 1 tsp dried oregano

1 bay leaf

salt and pepper

3 large aubergines, thinly
    sliced

6 tbsp butter

85 g/3 oz plain flour

600 ml/1 pint milk

1 egg, beaten

25 g/1 oz kefalotiri or
    pecorino cheese, grated

method

1 Heat 2 tablespoons of the olive oil in a large saucepan. Fry the onion and garlic until softened. Add the lamb and fry until browned, stirring frequently and breaking up the meat. Add the wine, tomato purée, sugar, cinnamon, oregano, bay leaf, salt and pepper. Bring to the boil, then simmer, uncovered, for 20 minutes, stirring occasionally.

2 Pour enough oil into a large frying pan to cover the bottom, heat and fry a layer of aubergine slices on both sides until lightly browned. Continue frying the aubergine in batches, adding more oil as necessary. Drain on kitchen paper.

3 To make the topping, put the butter, flour and milk in a saucepan and heat gently, whisking vigorously with a balloon whisk, until the sauce thickens, boils and is smooth. Simmer for 1–2 minutes. Remove from the heat and allow to cool slightly, then season with salt and pepper and whisk in the egg.

4 Arrange a layer of aubergine slices in the bottom of a large, ovenproof dish, then spoon over a layer of meat. Repeat until all the aubergines and meat have been used. Pour over the sauce, then sprinkle the grated cheese over the top.

5 Bake in a preheated oven, 180°C/350°F, for about 1 hour or until golden. Serve hot or warm.

lamb & potato moussaka

ingredients

SERVES 4

1 tbsp olive or vegetable oil

1 onion, chopped finely

1 garlic clove, crushed

350 g/12 oz lean minced
    lamb

250 g/9 oz sliced mushrooms

425 g/15 oz canned chopped
    tomatoes with herbs

150 ml/5 fl oz lamb or
    vegetable stock

2 tbsp cornstarch

2 tbsp water

1 large aubergine, sliced

500 g/1 lb 2 oz potatoes,
    parboiled for 10 minutes
    and sliced

2 eggs

115 g/4$\frac{1}{2}$ oz soft cheese

150 ml/5 fl oz natural yogurt

salt and pepper

55 g/2 oz kefalotiri or
    pecorino cheese, grated

fresh flat-leaf parsley,
    to garnish

salad leaves, to serve

method

1 Heat the oil in a saucepan and cook the onion and garlic for 3–4 minutes. Add the lamb and mushrooms and cook for 5 minutes, until browned. Stir in the tomatoes and stock, bring to the boil and simmer for 10 minutes. Mix the cornstarch with the water to a smooth paste and stir into the pan. Cook, stirring constantly, until thickened.

2 Spoon half the mixture into an ovenproof dish. Cover with the aubergine slices, then the remaining lamb mixture. Arrange the sliced potatoes on top.

3 Beat together the eggs, soft cheese and yogurt and season to taste with salt and pepper. Pour over the potatoes to cover them completely. Sprinkle with the grated cheese.

4 Bake in a preheated oven, 190°C/375°F, for 45 minutes or until the topping is set and golden brown. Garnish with flat-leaf parsley and serve with salad leaves.

lamb with tomatoes, artichokes & olives

ingredients

SERVES 4

4 tbsp authentic Greek yogurt

grated rind of 1 lemon

2 garlic cloves, crushed

3 tbsp olive oil

1 tsp ground cumin

salt and pepper

700 g/1 lb 10 oz lean
    boneless lamb, cubed

1 onion, sliced thinly

150 ml/5 fl oz dry white wine

450 g/1 lb tomatoes,
    chopped roughly

1 tbsp tomato purée

pinch of sugar

2 tbsp chopped fresh oregano
    or 1 tsp dried

2 bay leaves

85 g/3 oz kalamata olives

400 g/14 oz canned artichoke
    hearts, drained and halved

method

1 Put the yogurt, lemon rind, garlic, 1 table-spoon of the olive oil, cumin, salt and pepper in a large bowl and mix together. Add the lamb and toss together until coated in the mixture. Cover and marinate for at least 1 hour.

2 Heat 1 tablespoon of the olive oil in a large flameproof casserole. Add the lamb in batches and fry for about 5 minutes, stirring frequently, until browned on all sides. Using a slotted spoon, remove the meat from the casserole and set aside. Add the remaining tablespoon of oil to the casserole with the onion and fry for 5 minutes or until softened.

3 Pour the wine into the casserole, stirring in any glazed bits from the bottom, and bring to the boil. Reduce the heat and return the meat to the casserole, then stir in the tomatoes, tomato purée, sugar, oregano and bay leaves.

4 Cover the casserole with a lid and simmer for about 1 1/2 hours, until the lamb is tender. Stir in the olives and artichokes and simmer for another 10 minutes. Serve hot.

cinnamon lamb casserole

ingredients

SERVES 6

2 tbsp plain flour

pepper

1 kg/2 lb 4 oz lean boned
    lamb, cubed

2 tbsp olive oil

2 large onions, sliced

1 garlic clove, chopped finely

300 ml/10 fl oz full-bodied
    red wine

2 tbsp red wine vinegar

400 g/14 oz canned chopped
    tomatoes in juice

55 g/2 oz seedless raisins

1 tbsp ground cinnamon

pinch of sugar

1 bay leaf

salt

paprika, to garnish

topping

150 ml/5 fl oz authentic
    Greek yogurt

2 garlic cloves, crushed

salt and pepper

method

1 Put the flour and pepper in a plastic bag, add the lamb cubes and shake well to coat each piece.

2 Heat the oil in a large, flameproof casserole. Add the onions and garlic and fry until softened. Add the lamb to the casserole and fry for about 5 minutes, stirring frequently, until browned on all sides.

3 Pour in the wine, vinegar and tomatoes, stirring in any glazed bits from the bottom of the casserole, and bring to the boil. Reduce the heat and add the raisins, cinnamon, sugar and bay leaf. Season with salt and pepper.

4 Cover the casserole with a lid and simmer gently for 2 hours or until the lamb is tender.

5 Meanwhile, make the topping. Put the yogurt into a small serving bowl, stir in the garlic and season with salt and pepper. Chill in the refrigerator until ready to serve.

6 Serve the casserole hot, topped with a spoonful of the garlic yogurt and dusted with paprika.

lamb with aubergine & black olive sauce

ingredients

SERVES 4

4–8 lamb chops

salt and pepper

3 tbsp olive oil

1 aubergine, cut into 2-cm/
   ¾-inch cubes

1 onion, chopped coarsely

1 garlic clove, chopped finely

400 g/14 oz canned chopped
   tomatoes in juice

pinch of sugar

16 black Greek olives,
   preferably kalamata, pitted
   and chopped roughly

1 tsp chopped fresh herbs
   such as basil, flat-leaf
   parsley or oregano

method

1 Preheat the grill. Season the lamb chops with pepper.

2 Place the lamb chops on the grill pan and cook under medium heat for 10–15 minutes until tender, turning once during the cooking time.

3 Meanwhile, heat the olive oil in a saucepan, add the aubergine, onion and garlic and fry for 10 minutes or until softened and starting to brown. Add the tomatoes and their juice, the sugar, olives, chopped herbs, salt and pepper and simmer for 5–10 minutes.

4 To serve, spoon the sauce onto four warmed serving plates and top with the lamb chops.

lamb with courgettes & tomatoes

ingredients

SERVES 4

4–8 lamb chops
salt and pepper
2 tbsp olive oil
1 onion, chopped finely
1 garlic clove, chopped finely
4 tbsp ouzo (optional)
400 g/14 oz canned tomatoes
    in juice
pinch of sugar
250 g/9 oz courgettes, sliced
2 tbsp chopped fresh thyme

method

1 Season the lamb chops with pepper. Heat the oil in a large, flameproof casserole, add the onion and garlic and fry for 5 minutes or until softened. Add the lamb chops and fry until browned on both sides.

2 Stir in the ouzo, if using, then add the tomatoes with their juice, sugar, courgettes, thyme and salt.

3 Bring to the boil and then simmer for 30–45 minutes, stirring occasionally and turning the chops once during cooking, until the lamb and courgettes are tender. If necessary, add a little water during cooking.

4 Serve hot.

rosemary lamb in filo pastry

ingredients

SERVES 4

3 tbsp olive oil

1 small onion, chopped finely

1 garlic clove, chopped finely

175 g/6 oz fresh spinach
    leaves

pinch of freshly grated
    nutmeg

2 tbsp authentic Greek yogurt

salt and pepper

4 lamb fillets, each weighing
    about 115 g/4 oz

1 tsp finely chopped fresh
    rosemary leaves

60 g/2¹/₂ oz butter

8 sheets authentic Greek
    filo pastry (work with
    one sheet at a time and
    keep the remaining
    sheets covered with a
    damp tea towel)

method

1 Heat 2 tablespoons of the olive oil in a
heavy-based saucepan, add the onion and garlic
and fry for about 5 minutes or until softened. Add
the spinach leaves and nutmeg and cook for
3 minutes, stirring.

2 Turn the spinach mixture into a food
processor or blender, add the yogurt, salt and
pepper and blend until smooth. Let cool.

3 Meanwhile, heat the remaining tablespoon
of oil in a frying pan. Add the lamb fillets and
rosemary and fry for 3 minutes on each side.
Remove from the frying pan, drain on kitchen
paper and set aside to cool.

4 When the lamb fillets are cool, slash each
one 4 times, almost all the way through.
Fill each slash with the spinach mixture,
spreading any remaining mixture on top.
Season the fillets with salt and pepper.

5 Melt the butter. Take 1 sheet of pastry and
brush with a little of the melted butter. Place
a second sheet on top, brush with butter and
fold them in half. Put a lamb fillet in the
centre and wrap to form a parcel. Place on a
baking sheet and brush with butter. Repeat to
form 4 parcels.

6 Bake the lamb parcels in a preheated oven,
190°C/375°F, for 25 minutes or until golden.
Serve hot.

marinated lamb & vegetable kebabs

ingredients

SERVES 4

juice of 2 large lemons

100 ml/3½ fl oz olive oil

1 garlic clove, crushed

1 tbsp chopped fresh oregano
    or mint

salt and pepper

700 g/1 lb 9 oz boned leg or
    fillet of lamb

2 green peppers

2 courgettes

12 pickling onions, peeled
    and left whole

8 large bay leaves

lemon wedges, to garnish

rice, to serve

cucumber and yogurt dip,
    to serve (see page 14)

method

1 Put the lemon juice, oil, garlic, oregano or mint, salt and pepper in a bowl and whisk together. Trim and cut the lamb into 4-cm/1½-inch cubes and add to the marinade.

2 Toss the lamb in the marinade, cover and refrigerate overnight or for at least 8 hours. Stir occasionally to coat the lamb.

3 When ready to serve, core and deseed the peppers and cut into 4-cm/1½-inch pieces. Cut the courgettes into 2.5-cm/1-inch pieces. Thread the lamb, peppers, courgettes, onions and bay leaves onto 8 flat, greased metal kebab skewers, alternating and dividing the ingredients as evenly as possible. Place on a greased grill pan.

4 Preheat the grill then cook the kebabs for 10–15 minutes, turning frequently and basting with any remaining marinade, until cooked.

5 Serve hot, garnished with lemon wedges, with rice and a bowl of cucumber and yogurt dip.

smyrna sausages in tomato sauce

ingredients

SERVES 4

500 g/1 lb 2 oz lean, finely
    minced lamb
55 g/2 oz fresh breadcrumbs
1 onion, chopped very finely
1 garlic clove, crushed
3 tbsp finely chopped fresh
    flat-leaf parsley
1 tsp ground cumin
pinch of ground cinnamon
salt and pepper
1 egg, beaten
2 tbsp olive oil

tomato sauce

800 g/1 lb 12 oz canned
    chopped tomatoes in juice
1/4 tsp sugar
50 ml/2 fl oz olive oil
1 garlic clove, crushed
1/4 tsp ground cumin
1 tbsp chopped fresh
    flat-leaf parsley
1 bay leaf
salt and pepper

method

1 To make the sausages, put the minced lamb, breadcrumbs, onion, garlic, parsley, cumin, cinnamon, salt and pepper in a bowl and mix together.

2 Stir in the beaten egg, then knead the mixture for about 5 minutes or until it forms a paste. Chill in the refrigerator for about 1 hour.

3 Meanwhile, prepare the tomato sauce. Put all the ingredients in a large saucepan (it needs to be large enough to hold the sausages in a single layer). Bring to the boil, then simmer for about 30 minutes.

4 With dampened hands, form the lamb mixture into 12 equal-size sausage shapes, each about 9 cm/3 1/2 inches long. Heat the oil in a large frying pan, add the sausages and fry for 15 minutes or until browned on all sides.

5 Using a slotted spoon, transfer the sausages to the pan containing the tomato sauce and simmer for 10–15 minutes. Serve hot.

lamb's liver in red wine & orange sauce

ingredients

SERVES 4

2 oranges

8 thin slices lamb's or
    calf's liver

2 tbsp plain flour

1 tsp paprika

3 tbsp olive oil

175 ml/6 fl oz dry
    red wine

2 tbsp chopped fresh flat-leaf
    parsley, plus extra
    to garnish

2 tbsp chopped fresh oregano

salt and pepper

pasta, to serve

method

1 Using a zester, remove the zest from the oranges. Put the zest in a small saucepan of boiling water, boil for 1 minute, then drain and set aside. Squeeze the juice from the oranges and set aside.

2 Remove and discard any ducts and membrane from the liver slices. Put the flour and paprika in a plastic bag, add the liver and shake well to coat each piece.

3 Heat the oil in a large frying pan. Add the liver and fry over a medium heat for 4–5 minutes, stirring constantly, until lightly browned all over but still moist in the centre. Remove from the frying pan with a slotted spoon and place on 4 warmed serving plates.

4 Add the wine to the frying pan, stirring in any glazed bits from the bottom. Boil briskly for 1 minute. Reduce the heat and stir in the orange juice, parsley, oregano, salt and pepper. Heat gently until reduced slightly, then spoon over the liver and garnish with the reserved orange zest and parsley. Serve hot, with pasta.

pork & cos lettuce in egg & lemon sauce

ingredients

SERVES 4

4 pork loin steaks

salt and pepper

2 tbsp olive oil

bunch spring onions, white
     parts only, sliced thinly

1 cos lettuce, sliced thinly
     widthways

1 tbsp chopped fresh dill

225 ml/8 fl oz chicken stock

2 eggs

juice of 1 large lemon

method

1 Season the pork steaks with pepper. Heat the oil in a large, heavy-based frying pan, add the spring onions and fry until softened. Add the pork steaks and fry for 10 minutes, turning the steaks several times, until browned on both sides and tender.

2 When the pork steaks are cooked, add the lettuce, dill and stock to the frying pan. Bring to the boil, cover and then simmer for 4–5 minutes or until the lettuce has wilted.

3 Meanwhile, put the eggs and lemon juice in a large bowl and whisk together.

4 When the lettuce has wilted, remove the pork steaks and lettuce from the frying pan with a slotted spoon, put in a warmed serving dish and keep warm in a low oven. Strain the cooking liquid into a measuring jug.

5 Gradually add 4 tablespoons of the hot cooking liquid to the lemon mixture, whisking all the time. Pour the egg mixture into the frying pan and simmer for 2–3 minutes, whisking all the time, until the sauce thickens. (Do not boil or the sauce will curdle.) Season with salt and pepper. Pour the sauce over the pork steaks and lettuce and serve hot.

pork with fennel & juniper

ingredients

SERVES 4

1/2 fennel bulb

1 tbsp juniper berries

2 tbsp olive oil

finely grated rind and juice of
    1 orange

4 pork chops, about
    150 g/5 1/2 oz each

crisp salad, to serve

fresh bread, to serve

method

1 Finely chop the fennel bulb, discarding the green parts.

2 Grind the juniper berries with a pestle and mortar. Mix the crushed juniper berries with the fennel flesh, olive oil and orange rind.

3 Using a sharp knife, score a few cuts all over each pork chop. Place the chops in a roasting tin or ovenproof dish. Spoon the fennel and juniper mixture over the top. Pour over the orange juice, cover and marinate in the refrigerator for 2 hours.

4 Preheat the grill to medium. Cook the pork chops under the preheated grill for 10–15 minutes, depending on the thickness of the meat, or until the meat is tender and cooked through, turning occasionally.

5 Transfer the chops to serving plates and serve with a crisp, fresh salad and plenty of fresh bread to mop up the cooking juices.

braised pork with fennel

ingredients

SERVES 4

1 tsp fennel seeds

grated rind of 1 lemon

salt and pepper

4 pork chops

1 tbsp plain flour

2 tbsp olive oil

2 bunches spring onions,
    sliced thinly

1 garlic clove, chopped finely

2 fennel bulbs, sliced thinly
    with fronds snipped
    and reserved

250 ml/9 fl oz dry white wine

1 bay leaf

method

1 Crush the fennel seeds and mix with the lemon rind, salt and pepper. Spread the mixture over both sides of the pork chops and marinate for about 1 hour.

2 Dust the pork chops with the flour. Heat the oil in a flameproof casserole, add the pork and fry until browned on both sides. Remove from the casserole. Add the spring onions, garlic and fennel to the casserole and fry for 5–10 minutes or until softened and beginning to brown. Return the chops to the casserole.

3 Pour in the wine, stirring in any glazed bits from the bottom of the casserole, and bring to the boil. Reduce the heat and add the bay leaf. Cover the casserole with a lid and simmer for 45 minutes or until the pork chops are tender.

4 Serve sprinkled with the reserved snipped fennel fronds.

rabbit, roast tomato & sage pie

ingredients

SERVES 4

450 g/1 lb cherry tomatoes

3 tbsp olive oil

$^1/_2$ tsp sugar

700 g/1 lb 8 oz boned rabbit, cubed

1 tbsp plain flour

1 onion, chopped

1 garlic clove, chopped finely

3 tbsp pine nuts

150 ml/5 fl oz chicken or vegetable stock

1 tbsp lemon juice

12 fresh sage leaves, snipped finely

salt and pepper

3 tbsp butter

100 g/3$^1/_2$ oz authentic Greek filo pastry (work with one sheet at a time and keep the remaining sheets covered with a damp tea towel)

method

1 Put the tomatoes in a roasting tin and sprinkle with 1 tablespoon of the olive oil and the sugar. Roast in a preheated oven, 200°C/400°F, for 30 minutes.

2 Meanwhile, coat the cubes of rabbit in the flour. Heat 1 tablespoon of the oil in a large, heavy-based frying pan and fry the onion and garlic until softened. Add the pine nuts and fry for 1 minute. Using a slotted spoon, transfer the mixture to a 1.4-litre/2$^1/_2$-pint pie dish.

3 Add the remaining oil to the frying pan and fry the rabbit for 5–10 minutes or until browned on all sides. Add the stock and lemon juice, bring to the boil, then simmer for 2–3 minutes. Transfer the mixture to the pie dish. Gently stir in the roasted tomatoes. Add the sage and season with salt and pepper.

4 Reduce the oven temperature to 190°C/375°F. Melt the butter. Brush one sheet of pastry with butter, cut it into 1-inch/2.5-cm strips and arrange on top of the pie. Repeat with the remaining pastry sheets, arranging the strips on top of the pie in the opposite direction each time. Make sure the filling is covered and tuck in the edges.

5 Bake the pie in the oven for about 30 minutes or until golden brown. Serve hot.

roast chicken with oregano

ingredients

SERVES 4

1.6–1.8 kg/3½–4 lb whole
   chicken

1 lemon

4 tbsp chopped fresh oregano

1 garlic clove, crushed

2 tbsp butter

3 tbsp olive oil

salt and pepper

method

1 To calculate the cooking time, allow 20 minutes per pound plus 20 minutes.

2 Grate the rind from the lemon and cut the lemon in half. Put the chicken in a large roasting tin and squeeze the lemon juice from one lemon half into the cavity. Add the lemon rind, 3 tablespoons of the oregano and the garlic. Rub the butter, the juice from the remaining lemon half and the oil over the chicken. Sprinkle with the remaining oregano, salt and pepper. Put the squeezed lemon halves inside the chicken cavity.

3 Roast the chicken in a preheated oven, 190°C/375°F, for the calculated cooking time, basting occasionally, until golden brown and tender. (To test if the chicken is cooked, pierce the thickest part of a thigh with a skewer. If the juices run clear, it is ready.)

4 Allow the chicken to rest in a warm place for 5–10 minutes, then carve into slices or serving pieces. Stir the remaining juices in the pan and serve spooned over the chicken.

spicy aromatic chicken

ingredients

SERVES 4

4–8 chicken pieces, skinned

1/2 lemon, cut into wedges

4 tbsp olive oil

1 onion, chopped roughly

2 large garlic cloves, chopped
finely

125 ml/4 fl oz dry white wine

400 g/14 oz canned chopped
tomatoes in juice

pinch of sugar

1/2 tsp ground cinnamon

1/2 tsp ground cloves

1/2 tsp ground allspice

salt and pepper

400 g/14 oz canned artichoke
hearts or okra, drained

8 black Greek olives, pitted

method

1 Rub the chicken pieces with the lemon. Heat the oil in a large flameproof casserole or lidded frying pan. Add the onion and garlic and fry for 5 minutes or until softened. Add the chicken pieces and fry for 5–10 minutes or until browned on all sides.

2 Pour in the wine and add the tomatoes with their juice, the sugar, cinnamon, cloves, allspice, salt and pepper and bring to the boil. Cover the casserole and simmer for 45 minutes to 1 hour or until the chicken is tender.

3 Meanwhile, if using artichoke hearts, cut them in half. Add the artichokes or okra and the olives to the casserole 10 minutes before the end of cooking and continue to simmer until heated through. Serve hot.

chicken with walnut sauce

ingredients

SERVES 4

4–8 skinned chicken pieces

1/2 lemon, cut into wedges

3 tbsp olive oil

150 ml/5 fl oz dry white wine

300 ml/10 fl oz chicken stock

1 bay leaf

salt and pepper

100 g/3 1/2 oz walnut pieces

2 garlic cloves

150 ml/5 fl oz authentic
    Greek yogurt

chopped fresh flat-leaf
    parsley, to garnish

method

1 Rub the chicken pieces with the lemon. Heat the oil in a large frying pan, add the chicken pieces and fry quickly until lightly browned on all sides.

2 Pour the wine into the frying pan and bring to the boil. Add the stock, bay leaf, salt and pepper and simmer for about 20 minutes, turning the chicken several times, until tender.

3 Meanwhile, put the walnuts and garlic in a food processor and blend to form a fairly smooth purée.

4 When the chicken is cooked, transfer to a warmed serving dish and keep warm. Stir the walnut mixture and yogurt into the pan juices and heat gently for about 5 minutes until the sauce is fairly thick. (Do not boil or the sauce will curdle.) Season with salt and pepper.

5 Pour the walnut sauce over the chicken pieces and serve hot, garnished with chopped fresh parsley.

grilled chicken with lemon

ingredients

SERVES 4

4 chicken quarters

grated rind and juice of
    2 lemons

4 tbsp olive oil

2 garlic cloves, crushed

2 sprigs fresh thyme

salt and pepper

method

1 Prick the skin of the chicken quarters all over with a fork. Put the chicken pieces in a dish, add the lemon juice, oil, garlic, thyme, salt and pepper and mix well. Cover and marinate in the refrigerator for at least 2 hours.

2 To cook the chicken, preheat the grill or barbecue. Put the chicken in a grill pan or on the barbecue grill and baste with the marinade. Cook for 30–40 minutes, basting and turning occasionally, until the chicken is tender. (To test if the chicken is cooked, pierce the thickest part of the chicken pieces with a skewer. If the juices run clear, it is ready.)

3 Serve hot, with any remaining marinade spooned over and garnished with the grated lemon rind.

chicken with goat's cheese & basil

ingredients

SERVES 4

4 skinned chicken breast fillets

100 g/3^1/$_2$ oz soft goat's cheese

small bunch fresh basil

salt and pepper

2 tbsp olive oil

method

1 Using a sharp knife, slit along one long edge of each chicken breast, then carefully open out each breast to make a small pocket. Divide the cheese equally between the pockets and tuck three or four basil leaves in each. Close the openings and season the breasts with salt and pepper.

2 Heat the oil in a frying pan, add the chicken breasts and fry gently for 15–20 minutes, turning several times, until golden and tender.

3 Serve warm, garnished with a sprig of basil.

filo chicken pie

ingredients

SERVES 6–8

stock

1.5 kg/3 lb 5 oz whole
    chicken

1 small onion, halved,

1 carrot, sliced thickly

1 celery stalk, sliced thickly

pared rind of 1 lemon

1 bay leaf

10 peppercorns

155 g/5½ oz butter

3 large onions, chopped finely

55 g/2 oz plain flour

150 ml/5 fl oz milk

salt and pepper

25 g/1 oz kefalotiri or
    pecorino cheese, grated

3 eggs, beaten

225 g/8 oz authentic Greek
    filo pastry (work with one
    sheet at a time and
    keep the remaining
    sheets covered with a
    damp tea towel)

method

1 Put the chicken in a large saucepan with the halved onion, carrot, celery, lemon rind, bay leaf and peppercorns. Add cold water to cover and bring to the boil. Cover and simmer for about 1 hour, or until the chicken is cooked.

2 Remove the chicken and set aside to cool. Bring the stock to the boil and boil until reduced to about 600 ml/1 pint. Strain and reserve the stock. Cut the cooled chicken into bite-size pieces, discarding the skin and bones.

3 Fry the chopped onions until softened in 55 g/2 oz of the butter. Add the flour and cook gently, stirring, for 1–2 minutes. Gradually stir in the reserved stock and the milk. Bring to the boil, stirring constantly, then simmer for 1–2 minutes until thick and smooth. Remove from the heat, add the chicken and season to taste. Cool, then stir in the cheese and eggs.

4 Melt the remaining butter and use a little to grease a deep 30 x 20-cm/12 x 8-inch metal baking pan. Cut the pastry sheets in half widthways. Line the pan with one sheet of pastry and brush it with a little melted butter. Repeat with half of the pastry sheets. Spread the filling over the pastry, then top with the remaining pastry sheets, brushing each with butter and tucking down the edges.

5 Score the top of the pie into 6 or 8 squares. Bake in a preheated oven, 190°C/375°F, for about 50 minutes or until golden. Serve warm.

chicken kebabs with yogurt sauce

ingredients

SERVES 4

300 ml/10 fl oz authentic
    Greek yogurt
2 garlic cloves, crushed
juice of 1/2 lemon
1 tbsp chopped fresh herbs
    such as oregano, dill,
    tarragon or parsley
salt and pepper
4 large skinned, boned
    chicken breasts
8 firm stems of fresh
    rosemary, optional
shredded cos lettuce, to serve
rice, to serve
lemon wedges, to garnish

method

1 To make the sauce, put the yogurt, garlic, lemon juice, herbs, salt and pepper in a large bowl and mix well together.

2 Cut the chicken breasts into chunks measuring about 4 cm/1 1/2 inches square. Add to the yogurt mixture and toss well together until the chicken pieces are coated. Cover and marinate in the refrigerator for about 1 hour. If you are using wooden skewers, soak them in cold water for 30 minutes before use.

3 Preheat the grill. Thread the pieces of chicken onto 8 flat, greased, metal kebab skewers, wooden skewers or rosemary stems and place on a greased grill pan.

4 Cook the kebabs under the grill for about 15 minutes, turning and basting with the remaining marinade occasionally, until lightly browned and tender.

5 Pour the remaining marinade into a saucepan and heat gently but do not boil. Serve the kebabs with shredded lettuce on a bed of rice and garnish with lemon wedges. Accompany with the yogurt sauce.

fish & seafood

The sight of weathered fishermen in little boats landing their catch in a pretty harbour is undoubtedly one of the most appealing to a visitor to Greece. With so many miles of Mediterranean coastline at their disposal, it is hardly surprising that the Greeks feature fish and seafood prominently in their cuisine, and on long summer evenings those harbourside villages will have a tantalizing scent in the air of the day's catch being cooked.

The range of species is remarkable and includes sea bass, sea bream, monkfish, red mullet, mackerel and sardines as well as scallops, prawns, octopus and squid. They are cooked in a variety of appetizing ways – roasted, grilled, baked, pan-fried, deep-fried, barbecued, stuffed, wrapped in vine leaves – and are often served with classic Greek sauces such as garlic or egg and lemon. Other flavours, such as lemon or lime and wild oregano, complement the fish perfectly, and vegetables are often used in the dish – Traditional Greek Baked Fish, for example, is cooked on a bed of onions, carrots, celery, tomatoes and herbs. Seafood is also used to make a sauce for pasta, or added to a basic pilaf.

Many of the recipes in this section are suitable for adapting to different fish or seafood, so simply choose your favourite.

fish roasted with lime

ingredients

SERVES 4

1 kg/2 lb 4 oz white fish
   fillets, such as sea bass,
   flounder or cod

salt and pepper

1 lime, halved

3 tbsp extra-virgin
   olive oil

1 large onion, finely chopped

3 garlic cloves,
   finely chopped

2–3 pickled jalapeño chillies
   (jalapeños en escabeche),
   chopped

6–8 tbsp chopped fresh
   coriander

lemon and lime wedges,
   to serve

method

1 Place the fish fillets in a non-metallic bowl and season to taste with salt and pepper. Squeeze the juice from the lime halves over the fish.

2 Heat the oil in a frying pan. Add the onion and garlic and cook, stirring frequently, until softened. Remove the pan from the heat.

3 Place a third of the onion mixture and a little of the chillies and coriander in the bottom of a shallow ovenproof dish or roasting tin. Arrange the fish on top. Top with the remaining onion mixture, chillies and coriander.

4 Roast in a preheated oven, 180°C/350°F, for 15–20 minutes or until the fish has become slightly opaque and firm to the touch.

5 Serve at once, with lemon and lime wedges for squeezing over the fish.

grilled red snapper with garlic

ingredients

SERVES 4

2 tbsp lemon juice

4 tbsp olive oil, plus extra for
    greasing

salt and pepper

4 red snapper or mullet,
    scaled and gutted

2 tbsp chopped fresh herbs
    such as oregano, marjoram,
    flat-leaf parsley or thyme

2 garlic cloves, chopped finely

2 tbsp chopped fresh
    flat-leaf parsley

lemon wedges, to garnish

method

1 Preheat the grill. Put the lemon juice, oil, salt and pepper in a bowl and whisk together. Brush the mixture inside and on both sides of the fish and sprinkle on the chopped herb of your choice. Place on a greased grill pan.

2 Grill the fish for about 10 minutes, basting frequently and turning once, until golden brown.

3 Meanwhile, mix together the chopped garlic and chopped parsley. Sprinkle the garlic mixture on top of the cooked fish and serve hot or cold, garnished with lemon wedges.

traditional greek baked fish

ingredients

SERVES 4–6

5 tbsp olive oil, plus extra for
　　greasing
2 onions, sliced finely
2 garlic cloves, chopped finely
2 carrots, sliced thinly
2 celery stalks, sliced thinly
150 ml/5 fl oz dry white wine
400 g/14 oz canned chopped
　　tomatoes in juice
pinch of sugar
1 large lemon, sliced thinly
salt and pepper
2 tbsp chopped fresh
　　flat-leaf parsley
1 tsp chopped fresh marjoram
1–1.3 kg/2–3 lb fat whole
　　fish, such as sea bream,
　　bass, tilapia or red
　　snapper, scaled
　　and gutted

method

1 Heat 4 tablespoons of the oil in a large saucepan, add the onions and garlic and fry until softened. Add the carrots and celery and fry for 5–10 minutes or until slightly softened.

2 Add the wine and bring to the boil. Add the tomatoes and their juice, the sugar, lemon slices, salt and pepper and simmer for 20 minutes. Add the parsley and marjoram.

3 Put the fish in a greased, shallow ovenproof dish. Pour the vegetables around the fish, arranging some of the lemon slices on top. Sprinkle with the remaining oil and season with salt and pepper.

4 Bake the fish, uncovered, in a preheated oven, 180°C/350°F, for 45 minutes to 1 hour, depending on the thickness of the fish, until tender. Serve immediately.

roasted fish from spetsae island

ingredients

SERVES 4

2 tbsp olive oil, plus extra for
  greasing

1 onion, chopped finely

2 garlic cloves, chopped finely

100 ml/3$\frac{1}{2}$ fl oz
  dry white wine

400 g/14 oz canned chopped
  tomatoes in juice

pinch of sugar

2 tbsp chopped fresh flat-leaf
  parsley

salt and pepper

4 fish fillets, each weighing
  about 175 g/6 oz, such
  as sea bass, brill, turbot,
  cod, monkfish or tilapia

juice of $\frac{1}{2}$ lemon

55 g/2 oz dry white
  breadcrumbs

chopped fresh flat-leaf
  parsley, to garnish

method

1 Heat the oil in a frying pan, add the onion and garlic and fry for 5 minutes or until golden. Add the wine, the tomatoes and their juice, sugar, parsley, salt and pepper and bring to the boil, then boil gently for about 30 minutes or until the sauce has thickened. If necessary, increase the heat to reduce the liquid.

2 Meanwhile, put the fish in a greased ovenproof dish. Sprinkle with the lemon juice and season with salt and pepper.

3 When the tomato sauce has thickened, spread the sauce over the fish fillets. Roast in a preheated oven, 170°C/325°F, uncovered, for 10–15 minutes, depending on the thickness of the fish.

4 Increase the oven temperature to 220°C/ 425°F. Sprinkle the breadcrumbs on top of the fish. Return to the oven and roast for a further 15 minutes or until the fish is tender and the top light golden brown and crisp. Serve hot, garnished with chopped parsley.

red snapper wrapped in vine leaves

ingredients

SERVES 4

8 small fresh vine leaves or
    225-g/8-oz pack vine
    leaves preserved in brine
4 red snapper, each weighing
    about 200 g/7 oz, scaled
    and gutted
salt and pepper
1 lemon, sliced thinly and
    halved
small bunch fresh dill
2 tbsp olive oil

method

1 If using fresh vine leaves, tie them in bundles by their stalks and blanch them in boiling salted water for 1 minute. Rinse under cold running water, dry the leaves and cut out the stalks. If using preserved vine leaves, place them in a large bowl, add boiling water and leave to soak for 20 minutes. Drain, soak in cold water for 20 minutes and then drain again.

2 Season the fish cavities with salt and pepper, then insert some halved lemon slices and 2–3 sprigs of fresh dill in each. Brush the fish with the olive oil and season with salt and pepper.

3 Preheat the grill. Place 1 fish on 2 fresh, overlapping vine leaves or on 5–6 preserved vine leaves. Roll up the vine leaves and, if using fresh leaves, tie with string.

4 Grill the fish for about 10 minutes or until tender. Serve hot.

fish fritters with greek garlic sauce

ingredients

SERVES 4

115 g/4 oz plus 1 tbsp plain
flour, plus extra for dusting

pinch of salt

1 egg, beaten

1 tbsp olive oil

150 ml/5 fl oz warm water

675 g/1 lb 8 oz white fish
fillets, such as well-soaked
salt cod, monkfish or cod

sunflower oil, for deep-frying

lemon wedges, to garnish

1/2 quantity Greek garlic
sauce (see page 22)

radishes, to serve

method

1 To make the batter, put the flour and salt in a large bowl. Make a well in the centre and add the egg and oil, then gradually add the water, beating all the time, to form a smooth batter.

2 Discard any skin and bones from the fish fillets and cut the flesh into chunks, measuring about 5 cm/2 inches square. Dust lightly in flour so that the batter will stick to the fish when it is dipped in it.

3 Heat the oil in a deep-fat fryer to 180°C/350°F or until a cube of bread dropped into the fat turns brown in 1 minute. When the oil is hot, dip each piece of fish in the batter to coat, add to the hot fat in small batches and fry for about 5 minutes, depending on the thickness of the fish, until crisp and golden. Remove with a slotted spoon and drain on kitchen paper. Continue to cook the remaining fish in small batches.

4 Serve the fish fritters hot, garnished with lemon wedges and accompanied with the Greek garlic sauce and a bowl of radishes.

skate in mustard & caper sauce

ingredients

SERVES 4

2 skate wings

2 tbsp olive oil

1 onion, chopped finely

1 garlic clove, chopped finely

150 ml/5 fl oz authentic
    Greek yogurt

1 tsp lemon juice

1 tbsp chopped fresh flat-leaf
    parsley

1 tbsp capers, chopped
    coarsely

1 tbsp whole-grain mustard

salt and pepper

chopped fresh flat-leaf
    parsley, to garnish

lemon wedges, to serve

method

1 Cut each skate wing in half and place in a large frying pan. Cover with salted water, bring to the boil, then simmer for 10–15 minutes, until tender.

2 Meanwhile, make the mustard and caper sauce. Heat the oil in a saucepan, add the onion and garlic and cook for 5 minutes or until softened. Add the yogurt, lemon juice, parsley and capers and cook for 1–2 minutes or until heated through. (Do not boil or the sauce will curdle.) Stir in the mustard and season with salt and pepper.

3 Drain the skate and put on 4 warmed serving plates. Pour over the sauce and sprinkle with chopped parsley.

4 Serve hot, with lemon wedges.

roasted monkfish

ingredients

SERVES 4

675 g/1 lb 8 oz monkfish tail,
    skinned and boned
4–5 large garlic cloves, peeled
salt and pepper
3 tbsp olive oil
1 onion, cut into wedges
1 small aubergine, about 300 g/
    10½ oz, cut into chunks
1 red pepper, deseeded,
    cut into chunks
1 yellow pepper, deseeded,
    cut into chunks
1 large courgette, about
    225 g/ 8 oz, cut into
    chunks
1 tbsp shredded fresh basil

method

1 Make small slits in each monkfish fillet. Cut 2 of the garlic cloves into thin slivers and insert into the fish. Place the fish on a sheet of waxed paper, season with salt and pepper to taste and drizzle over 1 tablespoon of the oil. Bring the top edges together. Form into a pleat and fold over, then fold the ends underneath, completely encasing the fish. Set aside.

2 Put the remaining garlic cloves and all the vegetables into a roasting tin and sprinkle with the remaining oil, turning the vegetables so that they are well coated in the oil.

3 Roast in a preheated oven, 200°C/400°F, for 20 minutes, turning occasionally. Put the fish package on top of the vegetables and cook for a further 15–20 minutes or until the vegetables are tender and the fish is cooked.

4 Remove from the oven and open up the package. Cut the monkfish into thick slices. Arrange the vegetables on warmed serving plates and top with the fish slices.

5 Serve at once, sprinkled with the basil.

fish in egg & lemon sauce

ingredients

SERVES 6

6 fish steaks or fillets, each
    weighing about 200 g/7 oz
1 onion, sliced thinly
7 tbsp fresh lemon juice
150 ml/5 fl oz water
salt and pepper
3 eggs
1 tbsp chopped fresh dill

method

1 Put the fish in a large, shallow saucepan and add the onion slices, lemon juice, water, salt and pepper. Bring to the boil, cover the pan and simmer for 15–20 minutes or until the fish is tender.

2 Meanwhile, put the eggs in a bowl and whisk together. When the fish is tender, remove the fish and onions from the pan with a slotted spoon, put on a warmed serving dish and keep warm in a low oven.

3 Strain the liquid into a measuring jug, then very slowly add to the egg yolks, whisking all the time with a balloon whisk. Pour the liquid into a small saucepan and heat very gently for 2–3 minutes, whisking all the time, until the sauce thickens. (Do not boil or the sauce will curdle.)

4 Stir the dill into the sauce and season with salt and pepper. Spoon the sauce over the fish and serve hot or cold.

monkfish & prawn kebabs

ingredients

SERVES 4

600 g/1 lb 5 oz monkfish
1 green pepper
1 onion
3 tbsp olive oil, plus extra for
    greasing
3 tbsp lemon juice
2 garlic cloves, crushed
salt and pepper
16 large fresh prawns, peeled
16 fresh bay leaves

method

1 Cut the monkfish into chunks measuring about 2.5 cm/1 inch. Cut the pepper into similar-size chunks, discarding the core and seeds. Cut the onion into 6 wedges, then cut each wedge in half widthways and separate the layers.

2 To make the marinade, put the oil, lemon juice, garlic, salt and pepper in a bowl and whisk together. Add the monkfish, prawns, onion and pepper pieces and toss together until coated in the marinade. Cover and marinate in the refrigerator for 2–3 hours.

3 Thread the pieces of fish, pepper, onion and bay leaves onto 8 greased, flat metal kebab skewers, alternating and dividing the ingredients as evenly as possible. Place on a greased grill pan.

4 Preheat the grill then cook the kebabs for 10–15 minutes, turning frequently and basting with any remaining marinade, until cooked and lightly charred. Serve hot.

pan-fried fish with lemon

ingredients

SERVES 4

4 tuna or swordfish steaks,
    each weighing about
    200 g/7 oz

salt and pepper

3 tbsp olive oil

juice of 1 lemon

lemon wedges, to garnish

Greek garlic sauce, to serve
    (see page 22) (optional)

method

1 Put the fish steaks in a shallow dish and season with salt and pepper. Drizzle over 1 tablespoon of the oil and half the lemon juice. Cover the dish and leave to marinate in the refrigerator for at least 1 hour.

2 When you are ready to cook, heat the remaining oil in a frying pan or rub a little over a cast-iron griddle, add the fish steaks and fry for 3–8 minutes on each side, depending on their thickness, until tender. Do not overcook the fish or it will become dry.

3 Drizzle the remaining lemon juice over the fish steaks. Serve hot, garnished with lemon wedges and accompanied with Greek garlic sauce, if desired.

baked mackerel stuffed with raisins & pine nuts

ingredients

SERVES 4

3 tbsp olive oil

1 onion, chopped finely

100 g/3¹/₂ oz fresh
    breadcrumbs

55 g/2 oz raisins, chopped

100 g/3¹/₂ oz pine nuts

grated rind and juice of 1 lemon

1 tbsp chopped fresh dill

2 tbsp chopped fresh flat-leaf
    parsley

salt and pepper

1 egg, beaten

4 mackerel, each weighing
    about 350 g/12 oz, gutted

salad leaves, to serve

lemon wedges, to garnish

method

1 To make the stuffing, heat 2 tablespoons of the oil in a large, heavy-based frying pan, add the onion and fry for 5 minutes or until softened. Remove from the heat.

2 Put the breadcrumbs, raisins, pine nuts, lemon rind, dill, parsley, salt and pepper in a large bowl. Add the onion and egg and mix well together.

3 Press the stuffing mixture into the cavity of the fish and place in a greased, shallow ovenproof dish large enough to hold them in a single layer. Using a sharp knife, make diagonal slashes along each fish. Drizzle over the lemon juice and the remaining oil.

4 Bake the fish, uncovered, in a preheated oven, 190°C/375°F, for 30–45 minutes, basting twice during cooking, until tender. Serve hot, on a bed of salad leaves, garnished with lemon wedges.

fresh sardines baked with lemon & oregano

ingredients

SERVES 4

2 lemons

12 large fresh sardines, gutted

4 tbsp olive oil

4 tbsp chopped fresh oregano

salt and pepper

lemon wedges, to garnish

method

1 Slice 1 of the lemons and grate the rind and squeeze the juice from the second one.

2 Cut the heads off the sardines and place the fish in a shallow, ovenproof dish, large enough to hold them in a single layer. Place the lemon slices between the fish. Drizzle the lemon juice and oil over the fish. Sprinkle with the lemon rind and oregano and season with salt and pepper.

3 Bake in a preheated oven, 190°C/375°F, for 20–30 minutes or until the fish are tender.

4 Serve garnished with lemon wedges.

deep-fried seafood

ingredients

SERVES 4

corn oil, for deep-frying

200 g/7 oz white fish fillets, such as English sole, skinned and cut into strips

200 g/7 oz monkfish fillets, cut into bite-size chunks

4 live scallops, shucked and cleaned

225 g/8 oz large cooked prawns, peeled and deveined but with tails left intact

batter

115 g/4 oz plain flour

pinch of salt

1 egg yolk

1 tbsp olive oil

225 ml/8 fl oz milk

2 egg whites

to garnish

fresh flat-leaf parsley sprigs

lemon wedges

method

1 First, make the batter. Sift the flour with the salt into a bowl and make a well in the centre. Add the egg yolk and olive oil to the well and mix together with a wooden spoon, gradually incorporating the flour. Gradually beat in the milk to make a smooth batter. Cover and rest for 30 minutes.

2 Heat the corn oil in a deep-fat fryer or large, heavy-based saucepan to 180–190°C/350–375°F or until a cube of bread browns in 30 seconds.

3 Meanwhile, whisk the egg whites in a separate clean, greasefree bowl until they form stiff peaks. Gently fold into the batter.

4 Using tongs, dip the seafood, a piece at a time, into the batter to coat. Deep-fry in small batches for 3–4 minutes until crisp and golden (if you deep-fry too many pieces at a time, the oil temperature will drop and the batter will be soggy). Remove with a slotted spoon and drain on kitchen paper. Transfer to a warmed serving plate and keep warm in a low oven while you cook the remaining pieces.

5 Garnish with parsley sprigs and lemon wedges and serve.

seafood pasta

ingredients

SERVES 4

3 tbsp olive oil

1 onion, chopped

2 garlic cloves, chopped finely

100 ml/3^1/$_2$ fl oz dry white
  wine

400 g/14 oz canned chopped
  tomatoes in juice

pinch of sugar

2 tbsp chopped fresh herbs
  such as flat-leaf parsley,
  oregano or marjoram

salt and pepper

400 g/14 oz long, hollow
  Greek macaroni or other,
  short pasta

400 g/14 oz frozen seafood
  cocktail, thawed and
  drained

method

1 Heat 2 tablespoons of the oil in a large saucepan, add the onion and garlic and fry for about 5 minutes or until softened.

2 Pour the wine into the pan and bring to the boil. Add the tomatoes and their juice, the sugar, chopped herbs, salt and pepper and simmer for 15–20 minutes.

3 Meanwhile, cook the macaroni in a large pan of boiling salted water for 10–12 minutes or as directed on the packet, until tender. Drain the pasta and return to the pan. Add the remaining oil and toss together.

4 Add the seafood to the tomato sauce and simmer for 3–4 minutes or until heated through. Serve the seafood on top of the pasta.

pasta with scallops & pine nuts

ingredients

SERVES 4

400 g/14 oz long, hollow
    Greek macaroni or other,
    short pasta
4 tbsp olive oil
1 garlic clove, chopped finely
55 g/2 oz pine nuts
8 large scallops, sliced
salt and pepper
2 tbsp chopped fresh basil
    leaves

method

1 Cook the macaroni in a large saucepan of boiling salted water for 10–12 minutes or as directed on the packet, until tender.

2 About 5 minutes before the pasta is ready, heat the oil in a frying pan. Add the garlic and fry for 1–2 minutes until softened but not browned. Add the pine nuts and cook until browned. Stir in the scallops and cook until just opaque. Season with salt and pepper.

3 When the pasta is cooked, drain and return to the pan. Add the scallops and the juices in the frying pan to the pasta and toss together. Serve sprinkled with the chopped basil leaves.

prawn pilaf

ingredients

SERVES 4

3 tbsp olive oil

1 onion, chopped finely

1 red pepper, cored,
    deseeded and sliced thinly

1 garlic clove, crushed

225 g/8 oz long-grain
    white rice

700 ml//1¼ pints fish,
    chicken or vegetable stock

1 bay leaf

salt and pepper

400 g/14 oz peeled, cooked
    prawns, thawed and
    drained if frozen

to garnish

whole cooked prawns

lemon wedges

black Greek olives

to serve

grated kefalotiri or pecorino
    cheese

cubes of authentic Greek feta
    cheese

method

1 Heat the oil in a large, lidded frying pan, add the onion, red pepper and garlic and fry for 5 minutes or until softened. Add the rice and cook for 2–3 minutes, stirring all the time, until the grains look transparent.

2 Add the stock, bay leaf, salt and pepper. Bring to the boil, cover the pan with a tightly fitting lid and simmer for about 15 minutes or until the rice is tender and the liquid has been absorbed. Do not stir during cooking. When cooked, very gently stir in the prawns.

3 Remove the lid, cover the frying pan with a clean tea towel, replace the lid and stand in a warm place for 10 minutes to dry out. Stir with a fork to separate the grains.

4 Serve garnished with whole prawns, lemon wedges and black olives. Accompany with kefalotiri or pecorino cheese for sprinkling on top and a bowl of feta cubes.

made with
vegetables

Greek cuisine is ideal for the vegetarian or for those who simply love vegetables. The richly coloured vegetables that are now so firmly associated with the health-enhancing Mediterranean diet – aubergines, courgettes, peppers and tomatoes – flourish under the sunny Greek skies and form the basis for many tasty dishes. The Greeks also have creative ways of serving vegetables as side dishes – for example, carrots or shallots 'à la Grecque' ('in Greek style', cooked in a herb-flavoured liquid then chilled), fennel roasted with a crispy topping of breadcrumbs, or broad beans served as a salad with feta and spring onions in a lemon and olive-oil dressing.

Feta, the deliciously creamy, salty, goat's cheese of Greece, marries well with vegetable dishes, as does halloumi, a cheese with a curiously springy texture, which is made of sheep's and goat's milk, or sometimes also with cow's milk, and is especially delicious grilled or fried.

If you only try a few recipes from this section, go for the Spinach and Feta Pie, *spanakópita*, which is sold in various guises in all Greek bakeries, the Roasted Red Peppers with Halloumi recipe and of course the not-to-be-missed Greek Salad – an uncomplicated, fresh-tasting delight that simply says 'Greece'.

roasted vegetable moussaka

ingredients

SERVES 4–6

1 large aubergine, sliced
    thickly

2 medium courgettes, sliced
    thickly

2 onions, cut into small
    wedges

2 red peppers, cored,
    deseeded and chopped
    roughly

2 garlic cloves, chopped
    roughly

5 tbsp olive oil

1 tbsp chopped fresh thyme

salt and pepper

2 eggs, beaten

300 ml/10 fl oz authentic
    Greek yogurt

400 g/14 oz canned chopped
    tomatoes in juice

55 g/2 oz authentic Greek
    feta cheese

method

1 Put the aubergine, courgettes, onions, peppers and garlic in a roasting tin. Drizzle over the oil, toss together and then sprinkle over the thyme and season with salt and pepper. Roast in a preheated oven, 220°C/425°F, for 30–35 minutes, turning the tin halfway through the cooking, until golden brown and tender.

2 Meanwhile, beat together the eggs, yogurt, salt and pepper. When the vegetables are cooked, reduce the oven temperature to 180°C/350°F.

3 Put half the vegetables in a layer in a large ovenproof dish. Spoon over the canned chopped tomatoes and their juice, then add the remaining vegetables. Pour over the yogurt mixture and crumble over the feta cheese. Bake in the oven for 45 minutes to 1 hour, until golden brown. Serve hot, warm or cold.

vegetable moussaka

ingredients

SERVES 4

about 125 ml/4 fl oz olive oil

1 onion, chopped

4 celery stalks, chopped

1 garlic clove, finely chopped

400 g/14 oz canned chopped
tomatoes

300 g/10½ oz canned green
lentils

2 tbsp chopped fresh parsley

salt and pepper

1 large aubergine, sliced

sauce

2 tbsp butter

25 g/1 oz plain flour

300 ml/10 fl oz milk

salt and pepper

pinch of freshly grated nutmeg

1 egg

55 g/2 oz kefalotiri or
pecorino cheese, grated

method

1 Heat 1 tablespoon of the oil in a frying pan over medium heat. Add the onion and cook, stirring frequently, for 5 minutes or until softened. Add the celery, garlic, tomatoes, lentils and their can juices and parsley. Season to taste with salt and pepper. Reduce the heat, cover and simmer gently, stirring occasionally, for 15 minutes or until the mixture has thickened.

2 Meanwhile, heat a little of the remaining oil in a large, heavy-based frying pan. Add the aubergine slices, in batches if necessary, and cook until golden on both sides, adding more oil as necessary. Remove with a slotted spoon and drain on kitchen paper.

3 Layer an ovenproof dish with the lentil and tomato mixture and the aubergine slices, ending with a layer of aubergine.

4 To make the sauce, put the butter, flour and milk in a saucepan over medium-low heat and bring to the boil, whisking constantly. Season to taste with salt, pepper and nutmeg. Remove from the heat, cool slightly, then beat in the egg. Pour the sauce over the aubergine, sprinkle with the cheese and bake in a preheated oven, 180°C/350°F, for 30–40 minutes until golden on top.

5 Serve immediately.

stuffed cabbage leaves

ingredients

SERVES 4

8 large cabbage leaves
such as láhana, Chinese
leaves or Cos lettuce

800 g/1 lb 12 oz canned
tomatoes in juice

2 tbsp olive oil

2 onions, chopped finely

1 large garlic clove, chopped
finely

55 g/2 oz risotto or other
short-grain rice

85 g/3 oz sultanas

1 tbsp chopped fresh mint

300 ml/10 fl oz vegetable or
chicken stock

85 g/2 oz pine nuts

salt and pepper

1 tsp dried oregano

method

1 Plunge the cabbage leaves into a large saucepan of boiling water, return to the boil, then boil for 3–4 minutes until softened. Drain well, plunge into iced water then drain well again. If necessary, cut out any hard cores.

2 Chop 3 or 4 of the tomatoes into small pieces. Heat 1 tablespoon of the oil in a saucepan. Add half the onions and the garlic and fry until softened and browned. Stir in the chopped tomatoes, rice, sultanas and mint.

3 Add the stock, bring to the boil, then simmer for 15–20 minutes or until the rice is tender and the stock has been absorbed. Remove from the heat, stir in the pine nuts and season with salt and pepper.

4 To make the tomato sauce, heat the remaining oil in a pan, add the remaining onion and fry until softened and browned. Stir in the remaining tomatoes and their juice, the oregano, salt and pepper and bring to the boil, then simmer for about 10 minutes. Allow to cool slightly, then purée in a food processor.

5 Divide the stuffing mixture between the cabbage leaves and roll up and fold the leaves to form 8 neat packets. Place seam-side down, side by side, in a shallow ovenproof dish and pour over the tomato sauce. Cover the dish and bake in a preheated oven, 180°C/350°F, for 1 hour. Serve hot or warm.

stuffed courgettes with walnuts & feta

ingredients

SERVES 4

4 fat, medium courgettes

3 tbsp olive oil

1 onion, chopped finely

1 garlic clove, chopped finely

55 g/2 oz authentic Greek feta cheese, crumbled

25 g/1 oz walnut pieces, chopped

55 g/2 oz white breadcrumbs

1 egg, beaten

1 tsp chopped fresh dill

salt and pepper

method

1 Put the courgettes in a pan of boiling water, return to the boil and then boil for 3 minutes. Drain, rinse under cold water and drain again. Set aside to cool.

2 When the courgettes are cool enough to handle, cut a thin strip off the top side of each one with a sharp knife. Using a teaspoon, carefully scoop out the flesh, leaving a shell to hold the stuffing. Chop the courgette flesh.

3 Heat 2 tablespoons of the oil in a saucepan. Add the onion and garlic and fry for 5 minutes or until softened. Add the courgette flesh and fry for 5 minutes or until the onion is golden brown. Remove from the heat and cool slightly. Stir in the cheese then the walnuts, breadcrumbs, egg, dill, salt and pepper.

4 Use the stuffing to fill the courgette shells and place side by side in an ovenproof dish. Drizzle over the remaining oil.

5 Cover the dish with foil and bake in a preheated oven, 190°C/375°F, for 30 minutes. Remove the foil and bake for another 10–15 minutes or until golden brown. Serve hot.

baked stuffed aubergines

ingredients

SERVES 4

4 large, long, thin aubergines

4 tbsp olive oil plus
    150 ml/ 5 fl oz olive oil
    or sunflower oil

3 large onions, sliced thinly

2 large garlic cloves, chopped
    finely

1 green pepper, cored,
    deseeded and sliced thinly

400 g/14 oz canned tomatoes
    in juice, drained

1 tsp dried oregano

1/4 tsp dried thyme

4 tbsp chopped fresh flat-leaf
    parsley, plus extra to garnish

salt and pepper

2 tbsp lemon juice

method

1 Cut the aubergines in half lengthways. Scoop out the flesh, leaving a shell to hold the stuffing, and reserve. Roughly chop the scooped-out flesh.

2 Heat the 4 tablespoons of olive oil in a saucepan. Add the onions, garlic and green pepper and cook for 10–15 minutes until softened, stirring occasionally.

3 Add the aubergine flesh, the tomatoes, breaking them up with a fork, the oregano, thyme, parsley, salt and pepper. Simmer for 20–30 minutes until the mixture has reduced and thickened slightly.

4 Spoon the stuffing into the aubergine shells and place them, side by side, in a shallow ovenproof dish.

5 Pour the remaining oil around the aubergines. Add the lemon juice and enough boiling water to come halfway up the sides of the aubergines. Cover the dish and cook in a preheated oven, 150°C/300°F, for 1 hour or until tender. Set aside to cool in the liquid, but do not chill.

6 To serve, lift out the aubergines with a slotted spoon, discarding the liquid, and garnish with chopped parsley.

roasted red peppers with halloumi

ingredients

SERVES 6

6 small red peppers

2 tbsp olive oil, plus extra for
    greasing

3 garlic cloves, sliced thinly

250 g/9 oz halloumi,
    provolone, or feta cheese,
    sliced thinly

12 fresh mint leaves

grated rind and juice of
    1 lemon

1 tbsp chopped fresh thyme

3 tbsp pine nuts

pepper

method

1 Cut the peppers in half lengthways and remove the cores and seeds. Rub the skins of the peppers with a little of the oil, then arrange them, skin-side down, on a large greased baking sheet.

2 Scatter half the garlic into the peppers; add the cheese, then the mint leaves, lemon rind, remaining garlic, thyme, pine nuts and pepper. Drizzle over the remaining oil and the lemon juice.

3 Roast the peppers in a preheated oven, 200°C/400°F, for 30 minutes or until tender and beginning to char around the edges. Serve warm.

spinach & feta pie

ingredients

SERVES 6

2 tbsp olive oil

1 large onion, chopped finely

1 kg/2 lb 4 oz fresh young
    spinach leaves, washed or
    500 g/1 lb 2 oz frozen
    spinach, thawed

4 tbsp chopped fresh
    flat-leaf parsley

2 tbsp chopped fresh dill

3 eggs, beaten

200 g/7 oz authentic Greek
    feta cheese

salt and pepper

100 g/3^1/$_2$ oz butter

225 g/8 oz authentic Greek
    filo pastry (work with
    one sheet at a time and
    keep the remaining
    sheets covered with a
    damp tea towel)

method

1 To make the filling, heat the oil in a saucepan, add the onion and fry until softened. Add the fresh spinach, if using, with only the water clinging to the leaves after washing, or the frozen spinach and cook for 2–5 minutes or until just wilted. Remove from the heat and cool.

2 When the mixture has cooled, add the parsley, dill and eggs. Crumble in the cheese, season with salt and pepper and mix well.

3 Melt the butter and use a little to grease a deep 30 x 20-cm/12 x 8-inch baking tin. Cut the pastry sheets in half widthways. Take 1 sheet of pastry and use it to line the base and sides of the tin. Brush the pastry with a little of the melted butter. Repeat with half of the pastry sheets, brushing each one with butter.

4 Spread the filling over the pastry, then top with the remaining pastry sheets, brushing each with butter and tucking down the edges. Using a sharp knife, score the top layers of the pastry into 6 squares.

5 Bake in a preheated oven, 190°C/375°F, for about 40 minutes or until golden brown. Serve hot or cold.

courgette pie

ingredients

SERVES 6–8

2 tbsp olive oil

2 bunches spring onions,
   sliced thinly

50 g/1³/₄ oz risotto or other
   short-grain rice

175 ml/6 fl oz hot vegetable
   or chicken stock

750 g/1lb 10 oz courgettes,
   grated coarsely and left
   to drain in a colander for
   5–10 minutes

4 tbsp chopped fresh
   flat-leaf parsley

2 tbsp chopped fresh mint

3 eggs, beaten

100 g/3¹/₂ oz authentic Greek
   feta cheese

salt and pepper

100 g/3¹/₂ oz butter

200 g/7 oz authentic Greek
   filo pastry (work with
   one sheet at a time and
   keep the remaining
   sheets covered with a
   damp tea towel)

method

1 Heat the oil in a saucepan, add the spring onions and fry until softened. Add the rice and cook for 1 minute, stirring to coat in the oil.

2 Add the stock to the pan and simmer for about 15 minutes or until the stock has been absorbed and the rice is tender but still firm to the bite. Remove the pan from the heat and stir in the grated courgette. Set aside to cool.

3 When the mixture has cooled, add the parsley, mint and eggs. Crumble in the cheese, season with salt and pepper and mix well.

4 Melt the butter and use a little to lightly grease a deep 30 x 20-cm/12 x 8-inch baking tin. Cut the pastry sheets in half widthways. Take 1 sheet of pastry and use it to line the base and sides of the tin. Brush the pastry with a little of the melted butter. Repeat with half of the pastry sheets, brushing each sheet with butter.

5 Spread the courgette mixture over the pastry, then top with the remaining pastry sheets, brushing each with butter and tucking down the edges. Using a sharp knife, score the top layers of the pastry into 6–8 squares.

6 Bake the pie in a preheated oven, 190°C/ 375°F, for about 35 minutes or until golden brown. Serve hot.

courgette slices
with greek garlic sauce

ingredients

SERVES 4

450 g/1 lb baby courgettes

3 tbsp plain flour

olive oil, for shallow-frying

grated rind and juice
    of 1/2 lemon

salt and pepper

1/2 quantity Greek garlic
    sauce (see page 22)

method

1 Cut the courgettes lengthwise into 1/4-cm/ 1/4-inch thick strips. Dust with flour to coat.

2 Pour enough oil into a large frying pan to cover the bottom, heat, then add the courgettes and fry for 5–10 minutes until golden brown, stirring occasionally.

3 When cooked, add the lemon rind and juice and season with salt and pepper. Serve the courgettes hot, with the Greek garlic sauce spooned on top.

artichoke hearts with broad beans

ingredients

SERVES 4

4 tbsp olive oil

1 bunch spring onions, white
parts only, sliced thinly

450 g/1 lb frozen broad
beans

100 ml/3^1/$_2$ fl oz water

juice of 1 lemon

400 g/14 oz canned artichoke
hearts, drained and halved

2 tbsp chopped fresh dill

salt and pepper

method

1 Heat the oil in a large saucepan. Add the spring onions and fry for 5 minutes or until softened. Add the beans and stir to coat in the oil.

2 Pour in the water and lemon juice; bring to the boil and boil, uncovered, for 5 minutes.

3 Add the artichoke hearts to the pan and gently boil for 5 minutes or until the beans are tender and most of the liquid has evaporated. Add the dill and season to taste.

4 Serve hot.

carrots à la grecque

ingredients

SERVES 4

700 g/1 lb 9 oz young carrots
50 ml/2 fl oz olive oil
425 ml/15 fl oz dry white wine
1 tbsp Greek honey
2 sprigs fresh thyme
6 sprigs fresh parsley
1 bay leaf
2 garlic cloves, chopped finely
1 tbsp coriander seeds,
    crushed lightly
salt and pepper
chopped fresh herbs,
    to garnish

method

1 Cut the carrots in half and then into quarters to form fingers of equal thickness. Put the carrots and all the remaining ingredients except the chopped herbs in a large saucepan and bring to the boil, then simmer, uncovered, for about 20 minutes or until the carrots are tender.

2 Using a slotted spoon, transfer the carrots to a serving dish. Return the cooking liquid to the boil and boil until reduced by about half.

3 Strain the cooking liquid over the carrots and set aside to cool. When cool, chill in the refrigerator for 3–4 hours or overnight.

4 Serve at room temperature, garnished with chopped fresh herbs.

braised okra with tomatoes

ingredients

SERVES 4–6

450 g/1 lb okra
150 ml/5 fl oz
    white wine vinegar
3 tbsp olive oil
1 large onion, chopped
    roughly
1 large garlic clove,
    chopped finely
400 g/14 oz canned chopped
    tomatoes in juice
pinch of sugar
salt and pepper
chopped fresh flat-leaf
    parsley, to garnish

method

1 Trim off the tops and tails of the okra but do not cut into the flesh. Put in a bowl, pour over the vinegar and leave in a warm place for 30 minutes. Rinse the okra well under cold running water and drain.

2 Heat the oil in a large frying pan, add the onion and garlic and fry for 5–10 minutes until softened. Add the okra and fry for about 5 minutes, stirring occasionally, until beginning to brown.

3 Add the tomatoes with their juice, the sugar, salt and pepper, then simmer for 15–20 minutes or until the okra is tender and the sauce reduced slightly. Do not boil or the okra will burst.

4 Serve hot or cold, garnished with chopped fresh parsley.

greek country beans

ingredients

SERVES 4

175 g/6 oz white beans, such
as cannellini, black-eyed
beans or butter beans,
covered with water and
soaked overnight
100 ml/3^1/$_2$ fl oz olive oil
1 large onion, chopped
roughly
1 large garlic clove,
chopped finely
2 carrots, chopped finely
2 celery stalks, finely sliced
400 g/14 oz canned chopped
tomatoes in juice
pinch of sugar
1 tsp dried oregano
1 tbsp chopped fresh
flat-leaf parsley
salt and pepper
Greek olives, to serve
lemon wedges, to serve

method

1 Drain the beans, put in a saucepan and
cover with cold water. Bring to the boil, then
boil for 10 minutes. Drain and set aside.

2 Heat the oil in a saucepan, add the onion
and garlic and fry for 5 minutes or until
softened. Add the carrots and celery and fry
for another 10 minutes or until browned.

3 Add the beans, tomatoes, sugar, oregano
and parsley and enough boiling water to just
cover the beans. (Do not add salt at this stage
because it toughens the beans.) Bring to the
boil, then simmer for 1–1^1/$_2$ hours or until the
beans are really tender and the sauce is thick.
The beans should be coated in sauce, but add
a little extra water during cooking if the sauce
becomes too thick. (The time will vary, depending
on the type of bean and its age.) Season with salt
and pepper.

4 Allow to cool slightly before serving with olives
and lemon wedges.

crispy roasted fennel

ingredients

SERVES 4–6

3 large fennel bulbs
4 tbsp olive oil
finely grated rind and juice of
    1 small lemon
1 garlic clove, chopped finely
55 g/2 oz fresh white
    breadcrumbs
salt and pepper

method

1 Trim the fennel bulbs, reserving the green feathery fronds, and cut into quarters. Cook the bulbs in a large saucepan of boiling salted water for 5 minutes until just tender, then drain well.

2 Heat 2 tablespoons of the olive oil in a small roasting tin, add the fennel and turn to coat in the oil. Drizzle over the lemon juice. Roast the fennel in a preheated oven, 400°F/200°C, for about 35 minutes or until beginning to brown.

3 Meanwhile, heat the remaining oil in a frying pan. Add the garlic and fry for 1 minute, until lightly browned. Add the breadcrumbs and fry for about 5 minutes, stirring frequently, until crispy. Remove from the heat and stir in the lemon rind, reserved snipped fennel fronds, salt and pepper.

4 When the fennel is cooked, sprinkle the breadcrumb mixture over the top and return to the oven for another 5 minutes. Serve hot.

shallots à la grecque

ingredients

SERVES 4

450 g/1 lb shallots
3 tbsp olive oil
3 tbsp clear honey
2 tbsp garlic wine vinegar
3 tbsp dry white wine
1 tbsp tomato purée
2 celery sticks, sliced
2 tomatoes, deseeded
    and chopped
salt and pepper
chopped celery leaves,
    to garnish

method

1 Peel the shallots. Heat the oil in a large saucepan, add the shallots and cook, stirring, for 3–5 minutes or until they begin to brown.

2 Add the honey and cook over high heat for a further 30 seconds, then add the garlic wine vinegar and white wine, stirring well.

3 Stir in the tomato purée, celery and tomatoes and bring the mixture to the boil. Cook over high heat for 5–6 minutes. Season to taste and set aside to cool slightly.

4 Garnish with chopped celery leaves and serve warm. Alternatively, chill in the refrigerator before serving.

tomato pilaf

ingredients

SERVES 4

3 tbsp olive oil

1 onion, chopped finely

1 garlic clove, chopped finely

225 g/8 oz long-grain
    white rice

400 g/14 oz canned chopped
    tomatoes in juice

pinch of sugar

600 ml/1 pint chicken or
    vegetable stock

1 tsp dried mint

salt and pepper

2 tbsp pine nuts

lemon wedges, to serve

method

1 Heat the oil in a large, heavy-based saucepan, add the onion and garlic and fry for 5 minutes or until softened. Add the rice and cook for 2–3 minutes, stirring all the time, until the rice looks transparent.

2 Add the tomatoes with their juice, the sugar, stock, mint, salt and pepper. Bring to the boil, then cover the pan with a tightly fitting lid and simmer for about 15 minutes or until the rice is tender and the liquid has been absorbed. Do not stir during cooking. When cooked, gently stir in the pine nuts.

3 Remove the lid, cover the pan with a clean tea towel, replace the lid and leave in a warm place for 10 minutes to dry out. Stir with a fork to separate the grains.

4 Serve with lemon wedges to squeeze over.

traditional greek salad

ingredients

SERVES 4

6 tbsp extra-virgin olive oil

2 tbsp fresh lemon juice

1 garlic clove, crushed

pinch of sugar

salt and pepper

200 g/7 oz authentic Greek
feta cheese

1/2 head of iceberg lettuce or
1 lettuce such as Cos or
escarole, shredded
or sliced

4 tomatoes, quartered

1/2 cucumber, sliced

12 black Greek olives

2 tbsp chopped fresh herbs
such as oregano, flat-leaf
parsley, mint or basil

method

1 Make the dressing by whisking together the oil, lemon juice, garlic, sugar, salt and pepper in a small bowl. Set aside.

2 Cut the feta cheese into cubes about 2.5-cm/1-inch square. Put the lettuce, tomatoes and cucumber in a salad bowl. Scatter over the cheese and toss together.

3 Just before serving, whisk the dressing, pour over the salad leaves and toss together. Scatter over the olives and chopped herbs and serve.

salad of leaves
with lemon dressing

ingredients

SERVES 4

200 g/7 oz mixed baby salad
leaves such as lamb's
lettuce, spinach,
watercress and wild rocket

4 tbsp mixed chopped fresh
herbs such as flat-leaf
parsley, mint, coriander
and basil

about 4 tbsp extra-virgin
olive oil

juice of about $1/2$ lemon

1 garlic clove, crushed

salt and pepper

method

1 Wash the salad leaves and discard any thick stems. Dry and put in a salad bowl. Add the chopped herbs.

2 Make the dressing by whisking together the oil, lemon juice, garlic, salt and pepper in a small bowl. Taste and add more oil or lemon juice if necessary.

3 Just before serving, whisk the dressing. Pour over the salad leaves, toss and serve.

broad bean salad

ingredients

SERVES 4

6 tbsp extra-virgin olive oil

grated rind of 1 lemon and
    2 tbsp lemon juice

1 small garlic clove, crushed

pinch of sugar

pepper

1.3 kg/3 lb fresh young broad
    beans or 675 g/1$^{1}/_{2}$ lb
    frozen baby broad beans

150 g/5$^{1}/_{2}$ oz authentic Greek
    feta cheese

1 bunch spring onions, sliced
    thinly

2 tbsp chopped fresh dill
    or mint

2 hard-boiled eggs,
    cut into quarters

lemon wedges, to serve

authentic Greek yogurt, to serve

method

1 Make the dressing by whisking together the oil, lemon rind and juice, garlic, sugar and pepper in a small bowl. Set aside.

2 Shell the fresh broad beans, if using, and cook in boiling salted water for 5–10 minutes or until tender. If using frozen broad beans, cook in boiling salted water for 4–5 minutes. Drain the cooked beans and put in a salad bowl.

3 Whisk the dressing and pour over the beans while they are still warm. Crumble over the feta cheese, add the spring onions and toss together. Sprinkle with the chopped dill and arrange the egg quarters around the edge.

4 Serve warm with lemon wedges and a bowl of yogurt to spoon on top, if desired.

charred pepper salad

ingredients

SERVES 4-6

2 green peppers

2 red peppers

2 yellow peppers

$1/2$ tsp cumin seeds or 2 tbsp
    chopped fresh marjoram

5 tbsp extra-virgin olive oil

2 tbsp lemon juice

2 garlic cloves, crushed

pinch of sugar

salt and pepper

Greek olives, to garnish

method

1 Preheat the grill. Grill the peppers, turning frequently, until the skins are charred all over. Put the peppers in a bowl, cover with a damp tea towel and leave until cold.

2 When the peppers are cold, hold them over a clean bowl to collect the juices and peel off the skin. Remove the stem, core and seeds and cut the peppers into thin strips. Arrange the pepper strips on a flat serving plate.

3 If using cumin seeds, dry-toast them in a dry frying pan until they turn brown and begin to pop. Shake the pan continuously to prevent them from burning and do not allow them to smoke. Lightly crush the toasted seeds with a pestle and mortar.

4 Add the toasted cumin seeds or marjoram, the olive oil, lemon juice, garlic, sugar, salt and pepper to the pepper juices and whisk together.

5 Pour the dressing over the peppers and chill in the refrigerator for 3–4 hours or overnight. Serve at room temperature, garnished with olives.

tomato salad with fried feta

ingredients

SERVES 4

3 tbsp extra-virgin olive oil

juice of $1/2$ lemon

2 tsp chopped fresh oregano

pinch of sugar

pepper

12 plum tomatoes, sliced

1 very small red onion, sliced
very thinly

15 g/$1/2$ oz rocket leaves

20 black Greek olives

200 g/7 oz authentic Greek
feta cheese

1 egg

3 tbsp plain flour

2 tbsp olive oil

method

1 Make the dressing by whisking together the extra-virgin olive oil, lemon juice, oregano, sugar and pepper in a small bowl. Set aside.

2 Prepare the salad by arranging the tomatoes, onion, rocket and olives on 4 individual plates.

3 Cut the feta cheese into cubes about 2.5-cm/1-inch square. Beat the egg in a dish and put the flour on a separate plate. Toss the cheese in the egg, shake off the excess and then toss in the flour.

4 Heat the olive oil in a large frying pan, add the cheese and fry over medium heat, turning over the cubes of cheese until they are golden on all sides.

5 Scatter the fried feta over the salad. Whisk together the prepared dressing, spoon over the salad and serve warm.

orange & fennel salad

ingredients

SERVES 4

4 large, juicy oranges

1 large fennel bulb, very
    thinly sliced

1 mild white onion, finely
    sliced

2 tbsp extra-virgin olive oil

12 plump black olives, pitted
    and thinly sliced

1 fresh red chilli, deseeded
    and very thinly sliced
    (optional)

finely chopped fresh parsley

crusty bread, to serve

method

1 Finely grate the rind of the oranges into a bowl and set aside. Working over another bowl to catch the juice, use a small serrated knife to remove all the white pith from the oranges. Cut the oranges horizontally into thin slices.

2 Toss the orange slices with the fennel and onion slices in a large bowl. Whisk the oil into the reserved orange juice, then spoon over the oranges. Sprinkle the olive slices over the top, add the chilli, if using, then sprinkle with the orange rind and parsley.

3 Serve with crusty bread.

orange & olive salad

ingredients

SERVES 4

4 thick-skinned oranges

1 small red onion, sliced
very thinly

16 large black Greek olives,
pitted

2 tbsp extra-virgin olive oil

1 tbsp lemon juice

pinch of sugar

salt and pepper

lettuce leaves, to serve

chopped fresh herbs such
as flat-leaf parsley, mint
or dill, to garnish

method

1 Using a sharp knife, remove the peel and pith from the oranges, then cut the flesh into $1/2$-cm/$1/4$-inch-thick slices, discarding the seeds and white membrane. Put the oranges and any juice, onion slices and olives in a large bowl.

2 To make the dressing, whisk together the oil, lemon juice, sugar, salt and pepper and drizzle over the salad ingredients. Gently toss together, then chill in the refrigerator for 2–3 hours.

3 Serve in a shallow dish lined with lettuce leaves. Garnish with chopped fresh herbs.

something sweet

The 'something sweet' at the end of a Greek meal is usually a bowl of fresh, seasonal fruit and there is a truly fantastic selection to choose from – grapes, cherries, figs, apricots, peaches, oranges, tangerines, dates, loquats, apples, pears, melons, pomegranates and strawberries. Another favourite is the delicious, thick, creamy Greek yogurt served with a drizzle of honey and perhaps a sprinkling of crushed pistachio nuts or almonds. This combination is also made into a wonderful ice cream that is not too sweet.

However, the Greeks do love sweet things, and these are eaten during the day with coffee, or perhaps an hour or two after a meal, rather than as a 'dessert'. Cakes and biscuits also feature seasonal produce such as fruits and nuts, and many are topped with a honey and citrus-fruit syrup that creates an irresistibly soft, moist texture. Greek Walnut Pastries, *baklavás*, a spicy nut filling in a crisp pastry case steeped in honey syrup, are nothing short of legendary.

The Greeks particularly enjoy their sweet treats on festive occasions, so why not do as they do and make a batch of buttery Greek Shortbread Cookies which, once cooked, are left to wallow in a bath of icing sugar. They just melt in the mouth – divine!

Greek walnut pastries

ingredients

MAKES 12

100 g/3^1/$_2$ oz butter

350 g/12 oz cups walnut pieces, chopped finely

55 g/2 oz caster sugar

1 tsp ground cinnamon

^{1}/$_2$ tsp ground cloves

225 g/8 oz authentic Greek filo pastry (work with one sheet at a time and keep the remaining sheets covered with a damp tea towel)

225 g/8 oz Greek honey

2 tsp lemon juice

150 ml/5 fl oz water

method

1 Melt the butter and use a little to lightly grease a deep 25 x 17.5-cm/10 x 7-inch/ baking tin.

2 To make the filling, put the walnuts, sugar, cinnamon and cloves in a bowl and mix well.

3 Cut the pastry sheets in half widthways. Take 1 sheet of pastry and use to line the tin. Brush the sheet with a little of the melted butter. Repeat with half of the pastry sheets, then sprinkle with the walnut filling. Top with the remaining pastry sheets, brushing each with butter and tucking down the edges. Using a sharp knife, cut the top layers of the pastry into 12 diamond or square shapes.

4 Bake in a preheated oven, 220°C/425°F, for 10 minutes, then reduce the oven temperature to 180°C/350°F and bake for another 20 minutes or until golden brown.

5 Just before the pastries have cooked, make the honey syrup. Put the honey, lemon juice and water in a pan and simmer for about 5 minutes or until combined. Set aside.

6 When the pastries are cooked, remove them from the oven and evenly pour over the honey syrup. Set aside to cool. Before serving, cut the pastries along the marked lines again to divide into pieces.

walnut custard tarts

ingredients

SERVES 4

40 g/1^{1}/$_{2}$ oz butter

8 sheets authentic Greek filo
    pastry (work with
    one sheet at a time and
    keep the remaining
    sheets covered with a
    damp tea towel)

40 g/1^{1}/$_{2}$ oz walnut halves

150 g/5^{1}/$_{2}$ oz authentic Greek
    yogurt

4 tbsp Greek honey

150 ml/5 fl oz double cream

2 tbsp caster sugar

2 eggs

1 tsp vanilla essence

icing sugar, for dusting

authentic Greek yogurt,
    to serve

method

1 Melt the butter. Brush 4 deep 10-cm/
4-inch tartlet pans with a little of the butter.
Cut the sheets of filo pastry in half to make
16 rough squares.

2 Take 1 square of pastry, brush it with a little
of the melted butter and use it to line 1 of the
pans. Repeat with 3 more pastry squares,
placing each of them at a different angle. Line
the remaining 3 pans and place the pans on a
baking sheet.

3 To make the filling, finely chop 2 tablespoons
of walnuts. Put the yogurt, honey, cream,
sugar, eggs and vanilla essence in a bowl and
beat together. Stir in the chopped walnuts
until well mixed.

4 Pour the yogurt filling into the pastry cases.
Roughly break the remaining walnuts and
scatter over the top. Bake in a preheated oven,
180°C/350°F, for 25–30 minutes until the
filling is firm to the touch.

5 Let the tartlets cool, then carefully remove
from the pans and dust with icing sugar. Serve
with a bowl of yogurt.

fig, ricotta & honey tart

ingredients

SERVES 6

pastry

75 g/2½ oz cold butter,
    cut into pieces, plus extra
    for greasing
150 g/5½ oz plain flour
pinch of salt
25 g/1 oz ground almonds
cold water

filling

6 figs
100 g/3½ oz caster sugar
600 ml/1 pint water
500 g/1 lb 2 oz ricotta cheese
4 egg yolks
½ tsp vanilla essence
2 tbsp flower honey, plus
    1 tsp for drizzling

method

1 Lightly grease a 22-cm/9-inch loose-based fluted tart tin. Sift the flour and salt into a food processor, add the butter and process until the mixture resembles fine breadcrumbs. Tip into a large bowl, stir in the almonds and add just enough cold water to bring the dough together.

2 Turn out onto a floured work surface and roll out the pastry 7.5 cm/3 inches larger than the tin. Carefully lift the pastry into the tin and press to fit. Roll the rolling pin over the tin to neaten the edges and trim the excess pastry. Fit a piece of baking parchment into the tart case, fill with baking beans and chill for 30 minutes.

3 Remove the tart shell from the refrigerator and bake for 15 minutes in a preheated oven, 190°C/375°F, then remove the beans and paper. Return to the oven for 5 minutes.

4 Put the figs, half the sugar and the water in a pan and bring to the boil. Poach gently for 10 minutes, drain and cool.

5 Drain any liquid from the ricotta. Stir in the egg yolks and vanilla essence, add the remaining sugar and the honey and mix well. Spoon into the tart case and bake for 30 minutes.

6 To serve, cut the figs in half lengthways and arrange on the tart, cut-side up. Drizzle with the extra honey and serve at once.

honey & lemon tart

ingredients

SERVES 8–12

pastry

225 g/8 oz plus 3 tbsp
  plain flour
pinch of salt
1¹/₂ tsp caster sugar
150 g/5¹/₂ oz butter
3-4 tbsp cold water

filling

375 g/13 oz cottage cheese,
  cream cheese or ricotta
6 tbsp Greek honey
3 eggs, beaten
¹/₂ tsp cinnamon
grated rind and juice
  of 1 lemon
2 lemon slices, 1 divided into
  eighths, to serve

method

1 To make the pastry, put the flour, salt, sugar and butter, cut into cubes, in a food processor. Mix in short bursts, until the mixture resembles fine breadcrumbs. Sprinkle over the water and mix until the mixture forms a smooth dough. Wrap the pastry in waxed paper or foil and allow it to rest in the refrigerator for about 30 minutes.

2 Meanwhile, make the filling. If using cottage cheese, push the cheese through a sieve into a bowl. Add the honey to the cheese and beat until smooth. Add the eggs, cinnamon and lemon rind and juice and mix well together.

3 On a lightly floured surface, roll out the pastry and use to line a 23-cm/9-inch tart tin. Place on a baking sheet and line with baking parchment. Weigh down with baking beans and bake in a preheated oven, 200°C/400°F, for 15 minutes. Remove the parchment and beans and bake for a further 5 minutes or until the base is firm but not brown.

4 Reduce the oven temperature to 180°C/350°F. Pour the filling into the pastry case and bake in the oven for about 30 minutes until set. Decorate with the lemon slices and serve cold.

orange cheesecake with caramelized lemon slices

ingredients

SERVES 8

butter, for greasing

350 g/12 oz cottage cheese
   or ricotta cheese

4 egg yolks

115 g/4 oz caster sugar

finely grated rind of 1 orange

50 ml/2 fl oz fresh orange
   juice

55 g/2 oz ground almonds

authentic Greek yogurt,
   to serve

caramelized lemons

2 lemons, sliced thinly

125 g/4½ oz caster sugar

150 ml/5 fl oz water

method

1 Grease the base of a 20-cm/8-inch cake tin with removable sides and line the tin with waxed paper.

2 If using cottage cheese, push the cheese through a sieve into a bowl. Gradually beat the egg yolks into the cheese, then add the sugar, orange rind and orange juice and beat until smooth. Carefully fold in the ground almonds.

3 Turn the mixture into the prepared tin and bake in a preheated oven, 180°C/350°F, for about 35 minutes or until set. When cooked, turn off the oven, open the oven door and leave ajar. Allow the cheesecake to remain in the oven for 2–3 hours to cool.

4 Meanwhile, make the caramelized lemons. Put the lemon slices, discarding any seeds, the sugar and the water in a small saucepan and bring to the boil, then simmer for about 45 minutes, shaking the pan occasionally, until most of the liquid has evaporated and the lemons have caramelized. Watch very carefully towards the end of cooking that the lemons do not burn. Drain the lemon slices on a wire rack.

5 When the cheesecake has cooled, carefully remove from the pan and decorate with the caramelized lemons. Serve accompanied with Greek yogurt.

greek rice pudding

ingredients

SERVES 4

125 g/4¹/₂ oz short-grain rice

300 ml/10 fl oz water

1 tbsp cornflour

600 ml/1 pint whole milk

85 g/3 oz caster sugar

1 tsp vanilla essence or finely
   grated rind of 1 large lemon

ground cinnamon,
   to decorate

method

1 Put the rice in a saucepan and add the water. Bring to the boil, then simmer for 12–15 minutes, stirring occasionally, until the water has been absorbed. Meanwhile, in a small bowl, blend the cornflour with 2 tablespoons of the milk.

2 Add the remaining milk to the rice, return to the boil, then simmer for 20–25 minutes, stirring frequently, until the rice is very soft and most of the liquid has been absorbed. Stir in the sugar, vanilla essence or lemon rind and the cornflour mixture, return to the boil, then simmer for another 5 minutes, stirring.

3 Spoon the rice mixture into individual serving dishes and set aside to cool. Serve cold, sprinkled generously with cinnamon.

doughnuts in honey syrup

ingredients

SERVES 6

300 g/10^1/$_2$ oz plain flour
1 tsp salt
finely grated rind of 1 orange
1 sachet easy-blend
    dried yeast
300 ml/10 fl oz warm water
125 ml/4 fl oz Greek honey
1 tsp lemon juice
sunflower oil, for deep-frying
ground cinnamon,
    to decorate

method

1 Put the flour, salt and orange rind in the bowl of an electric mixer fitted with a dough hook and sprinkle in the yeast. Gradually add the water and mix for 10 minutes to form a thick batter. Alternatively, make the batter in a large bowl using a whisk.

2 Cover the bowl with a clean tea towel and leave in a warm place for 2 hours or until risen with lots of bubbles.

3 Meanwhile, make the honey syrup. Put the honey, lemon juice and 1 tablespoon of water in a saucepan and simmer until combined. Set aside.

4 When the batter has risen, heat the oil in a deep-fat fryer to 180°C/350°F or until a cube of bread dropped into the fat turns brown in 1 minute. Using 2 teaspoons (one to scoop and one to push), dip the spoons in cold water to prevent the batter from sticking and drop small amounts of the batter into the hot oil. Cook about 5 at a time, for 2–3 minutes, turning with a slotted spoon, until they puff up and are golden brown. Remove from the fryer and drain on kitchen paper.

5 Serve about 5 hot doughnuts per person, spoon over the warm honey syrup and sprinkle with cinnamon.

apricot & pistachio cake

ingredients

SERVES 8–10

100 g/3¹/₂ oz ready-to-eat
    dried apricots

finely grated rind and juice
    of 1 large orange

175 g/6 oz butter, plus extra
    for greasing

175 g/6 oz caster sugar

4 eggs, separated

225 g/8 oz fine ground
    semolina

100 g/3¹/₂ oz ground almonds

syrup

150 g/5¹/₂ oz Greek honey

100 ml/3¹/₂ fl oz orange juice

2 tsp lemon juice

topping

300 g/10¹/₂ oz authentic
    Greek yogurt

50 g/1³/₄ oz shelled unsalted
    pistachio nuts, chopped.

method

1 Put the apricots, orange rind and orange juice in a bowl and soak for 12 hours. Transfer the apricots and juice to a food processor and blend until smooth.

2 Grease and line a 23-cm/9-inch round cake tin with removable sides with waxed paper.

3 Put the butter and sugar in a large bowl and beat together until light and fluffy. Add the egg yolks, one at a time, beating well after each addition. Add the semolina and ground almonds and mix well together. Fold in the apricot purée.

4 Whisk the egg whites until stiff, then fold into the mixture. Turn the mixture into the prepared tin and bake in a preheated oven, 180°C/350°F, for about 45 minutes or until light golden brown and firm to the touch.

5 Meanwhile, make the syrup. Put the honey, orange juice and lemon juice in a saucepan, bring to the boil, then simmer for 2–3 minutes or until combined. Set aside.

6 When the cake is cooked, let it stand in the tin for 5 minutes, then transfer to a wire rack set over a baking sheet. Prick the top of the cake all over with a fine skewer. If necessary, reheat the syrup. Spoon the hot syrup over the warm cake and leave on the wire rack to cool. Just before serving, spread the yogurt over the cake and sprinkle with the pistachio nuts.

walnut cake

ingredients

SERVES 12

115 g/4 oz plus 2 tbsp
self-raising flour
$^1/_2$ tsp ground cinnamon
$^1/_4$ tsp ground cloves
115 g/4 oz butter, softened,
plus extra for greasing
115 g/4 oz caster sugar
4 eggs
225 g/8 oz walnut pieces,
chopped finely
pared rind and juice of
1 orange
115 g/4 oz white granulated
sugar
2 tbsp brandy

method

1 Grease and line the bottom of a deep metal baking tin, measuring 25 cm x 17.5 cm/ 10 x 7 inches, with waxed paper.

2 Sift together the flour, cinnamon and cloves. Put the butter and caster sugar in a large bowl and beat together until light and fluffy. Add the eggs, one at a time, beating well after each addition. Using a metal spoon, fold in the sifted flour, then fold in the walnuts.

3 Turn the mixture into the prepared tin and bake in a preheated oven, 190°C/375°F, for 30 minutes or until risen and firm to the touch.

4 Meanwhile, put the orange juice in a measuring jug and add water to make 150 ml/ 5 fl oz. Pour into a saucepan, add the granulated sugar and the pared orange rind and heat gently until the sugar has dissolved. Bring to the boil and boil for 6 minutes or until the mixture begins to thicken. Remove from the heat and stir in the brandy.

5 When the cake is cooked, prick the surface all over with a fine skewer, then strain the hot syrup over the top of the cake. Leave in the tin for at least 4 hours before serving.

yogurt cake

ingredients

SERVES 8

150 ml/5 fl oz authentic
    Greek yogurt
140 ml/4$^{1}/_{2}$ fl oz sunflower or
    corn oil, plus extra for
    greasing
250 g/9 oz caster sugar
250 g/9 oz self-raising flour
2 eggs
finely grated rind and juice of
    2 large lemons
70 g/2$^{1}/_{2}$ oz white granulated
    sugar
2 tbsp Greek honey
25 g/1 oz toasted flaked
    almonds, to decorate
authentic Greek yogurt,
    to serve

method

1 Grease a 20-cm/8-inch round cake tin with removable sides and line with waxed paper.

2 Put the yogurt, oil, caster sugar, flour, eggs and lemon rind in a large bowl or food processor and whisk together until smooth.

3 Turn the mixture into the prepared cake tin and bake in a preheated oven, 180°C/350°F, for about 1$^{1}/_{4}$ hours, until golden brown and a skewer inserted in the centre comes out clean.

4 Meanwhile, put the lemon juice and granulated sugar in a saucepan and heat gently until the sugar has dissolved. Bring to the boil, then simmer for 2–3 minutes. Stir in the honey.

5 When the cake is cooked, carefully remove from the tin and place on a wire cooling rack set over a baking sheet. Prick the top of the cake all over with a fine skewer. If necessary, reheat the lemon syrup, then pour the hot syrup over the warm cake and set aside to cool. Scatter the flaked almonds on top to decorate before serving. Serve with Greek yogurt.

semolina & almond cake

ingredients

SERVES 8–12

225 g/8 oz butter, softened
225 g/8 oz caster sugar
6 eggs, separated
115 g/4 oz fine ground
   semolina
175 g/6 oz ground almonds
finely grated rind and juice of
   3 oranges
125 g/4½ oz white
   granulated sugar
50 ml/2 fl oz water
1 cinnamon stick
finely grated rind and juice of
   2 lemons

method

1 Grease a 23-cm/9-inch round cake tin with removable sides and line with waxed paper.

2 Put the butter and caster sugar in a large bowl and beat together until light and fluffy. Add the egg yolks, one at a time, beating well after each addition. Add the semolina, ground almonds, orange rind and orange juice and mix well together.

3 Whisk the egg whites until stiff, then fold into the mixture. Turn the mixture into the prepared tin and bake in a preheated oven, 180°C/350°F, for 50 minutes to 1 hour or until golden brown and firm to the touch.

4 Put the granulated sugar, the water and the cinnamon stick in a saucepan and heat gently until the sugar has dissolved. Bring to the boil and boil for 4 minutes or until the mixture begins to thicken. Remove from the heat and add the lemon rind. Strain in the lemon juice.

5 When the cake is cooked, let it stand in the tin for 5 minutes, then carefully remove and place on a wire cooling rack set over a baking sheet. Prick the top of the cake all over with a fine skewer. Remove the cinnamon stick from the lemon syrup and, if necessary, reheat the syrup. Spoon the hot syrup and lemon rind over the warm cake and cool before serving.

orange & walnut cakes

ingredients

MAKES ABOUT 18

400 g/14 oz self-raising flour
1/2 tsp bicarbonate of soda
1/2 tsp ground cinnamon
1/4 tsp ground cloves
pinch of grated nutmeg
pinch of salt
300 ml/10 fl oz olive oil
75 g/2³/4 oz caster sugar
finely grated rind and juice of
    1 large orange

topping

25 g/1 oz walnut pieces,
    chopped finely
1/2 tsp ground cinnamon

syrup

175 g/6 oz Greek honey
125 ml/4 fl oz water
juice of 1 small lemon
juice of 1 small orange or
    1 tbsp orange flower water

method

1 Sift together the flour, bicarbonate of soda, cinnamon, cloves, nutmeg and salt.

2 Put the oil and sugar in a bowl and beat together. Add the orange rind and juice, then gradually beat in the flour mixture. Turn the mixture onto a lightly floured surface and knead for 2–3 minutes or until smooth.

3 Take small, egg-size pieces of dough and shape into ovals. Place on baking sheets, allowing room for spreading and, with the back of a fork, press the top of each twice to make a criss-cross design.

4 Bake the cakes in a preheated oven, 180°C/350°F, for about 20 minutes or until lightly browned. Transfer to a wire rack to cool.

5 Meanwhile, make the topping by mixing together the chopped walnuts and cinnamon. To make the syrup, put the honey and water in a saucepan, bring to the boil, then simmer for 5 minutes. Remove from the heat and add the lemon juice and orange juice or orange flower water.

6 When the cakes have almost cooled, using a slotted spoon submerge each cake in the hot syrup and leave for about 1 minute. Place on a tray and top each with the walnut mixture. Cool completely before serving.

butter biscuits

ingredients

MAKES ABOUT 36

175 g/6 oz butter

140 g/5oz caster sugar

1 egg

280 g/10 oz self-raising flour

finely grated rind of 1 lemon

3 tbsp flaked almonds
    (optional)

method

1 Put the butter and sugar in a bowl and whisk until light and fluffy. Whisk in the egg, then fold in the flour and lemon rind.

2 Turn out the dough onto a lightly floured work surface and knead gently until smooth. Form the mixture into rolls the thickness of a finger, then cut into 10-cm/4-inch lengths. Shape each roll into an S-shape and place on baking sheets, allowing room for spreading. If desired, stud with a few flaked almonds.

3 Bake the biscuits in a preheated oven, 180°C/350°F, for about 15 minutes or until lightly browned. Cool on a wire rack. Store the biscuits in an airtight tin.

greek shortbread biscuits

ingredients

MAKES 24

225 g/8 oz butter, softened
55 g/2 oz icing sugar
1 egg yolk
1 tbsp ouzo or brandy
350 g/12 oz plain flour
115 g/4 oz ground almonds
icing sugar, for dredging

method

1 Put the butter and icing sugar in a large bowl and beat until pale and fluffy. Beat in the egg yolk and ouzo or brandy and then the flour and almonds to form a soft, firm dough. Using your hands, quickly knead the mixture together.

2 Cut the dough into 24 pieces. Roll each piece into a ball and then into a sausage shape measuring about 7.5 cm/3 inches long. Place the sausage over one finger and press down on the ends to form a plump moon shape. Place on baking sheets, allowing room for them to spread slightly.

3 Bake in a preheated oven, 180°C/350°F, for 15 minutes or until firm to the touch and light golden brown. Meanwhile, sift a layer of icing sugar into a large roasting tin.

4 When baked, allow the biscuits to cool slightly then place in the tin in a single layer, as close together as possible. Sift icing sugar generously on top and cool for 3–4 hours. Store them in an airtight tin with any remaining icing sugar, so that the biscuits remain coated.

pistachio ice cream

ingredients

SERVES 4

300 ml/10 fl oz double cream
150 g/5¹/₂ oz authentic Greek
   yogurt
2 tbsp milk
3 tbsp Greek honey
green food colouring
50 g/1³/₄ oz shelled unsalted
   pistachio nuts, finely
   chopped

pistachio praline
oil, for brushing
150 g/5¹/₂ oz granulated
   sugar
3 tbsp water
50 g/1³/₄ oz shelled, whole,
   unsalted pistachio nuts

method

1 Set the freezer to its lowest setting. Put the cream, yogurt, milk and honey in a bowl and mix together. Add a few drops of green food colouring to tint the mixture pale green and stir in well. Pour the mixture into a shallow freezer container and freeze, uncovered, for 1–2 hours, until beginning to set around the edges. Turn the mixture into a bowl and, with a fork, stir until smooth then stir in the pistachio nuts. Return to the freezer container, cover and freeze for a further 2–3 hours, until firm. Alternatively, use an ice cream maker, following the manufacturer's instructions.

2 To make the pistachio praline, brush a baking sheet with oil. Put the sugar and water in a saucepan and heat gently, stirring, until the sugar has dissolved, then let it bubble gently, without stirring, for 6–10 minutes or until lightly golden brown.

3 Remove the pan from the heat and stir in the pistachio nuts. Immediately pour the mixture onto the baking sheet and spread out evenly. Let it stand in a cool place for about 1 hour or until cold and hardened, then put it in a plastic bag and crush with a hammer.

4 About 30 minutes before serving, remove the ice cream from the freezer and let it stand at room temperature to soften slightly. To serve, scatter the praline over the ice cream.

lemon ice cream

ingredients

SERVES 4–6

ice bowl
2 lemons
water

ice cream
500 g/1 lb 2 oz authentic
    Greek yogurt
150 ml/5 fl oz double cream
115 g/4 oz caster sugar
6 tbsp lemon juice

method

1 To make the ice bowl, thinly slice the lemons and discard the pips. Use the lemon slices to line the base and sides of a 1.7-litre/3-pint freezerproof bowl. Insert a 1.1-litre/2-pint freezerproof bowl inside and fill the space between the two bowls with water. Immediately place a plate and heavy weight on top. Transfer to the freezer and freeze for at least 4 hours, until frozen.

2 Set the freezer to its lowest setting. To make the ice cream, put the yogurt, cream, sugar and lemon juice in a bowl and mix well.

3 Pour the mixture into a shallow freezer container and freeze, uncovered, for 1–2 hours or until beginning to set around the edges. Turn the mixture into a bowl and, with a fork, stir until smooth. Return to the freezer container, cover and freeze for another 2–3 hours or until firm. Alternatively, use an ice cream maker, following the manufacturer's instructions.

4 To use the ice bowl, remove the weight and plate and quickly run the bowls under hot water until they loosen, then remove the ice bowl. Quickly transfer the ice bowl to a serving plate and return to the freezer.

5 About 30 minutes before serving the ice cream, remove it from the freezer and leave at room temperature to allow it to soften slightly.

baked stuffed honey figs

ingredients

SERVES 4

150 ml/5 fl oz fresh orange
juice

6 tbsp Greek honey

12 no-soak dried figs

40 g/1^1/$_2$ oz shelled pistachio
nuts, chopped finely

25 g/1 oz no-soak dried
apricots, chopped very
finely

1 tsp sesame seeds

authentic Greek yogurt,
to serve

method

1 Put the orange juice and 5 tablespoons of
the honey in a saucepan and heat gently until
the honey has dissolved. Add the figs and
simmer for 10 minutes or until softened.
Remove from the heat and cool the figs
in the liquid.

2 Meanwhile, prepare the filling. Put the nuts,
apricots, sesame seeds and remaining
tablespoon of honey in a bowl and mix well.

3 Using a slotted spoon, remove the figs from
the cooking liquid and reserve. Cut a slit at the
top of each fig, where the stem joins. Using
your fingers, plump up the figs and stuff each
fig with about 1 teaspoon of the filling mixture.
Close the top of each fig and place in an
ovenproof dish. Pour over the reserved
cooking liquid.

4 Bake the figs in a preheated oven, 180°C/
350°F, for 10 minutes or until hot. Serve warm
or cold, with the sauce and Greek yogurt.

almond paste pears

ingredients

MAKES ABOUT 20

oil, for greasing

200 g/7 oz ground almonds

100 g/3¹/₂ oz caster sugar

2 tbsp fine ground semolina

1 egg, beaten

1 tsp orange flower water or
    rosewater, plus extra for
    brushing

about 20 whole cloves

icing sugar, for dusting

method

1 Oil a baking sheet. Put the ground almonds, caster sugar and semolina in a bowl and mix together. Stir in the egg and orange-flower water or rosewater and knead to a smooth dough.

2 Break off small pieces of the mixture, about the size of a walnut, and form into pear shapes. Insert a clove in the top of each to form a stem. Place on the baking sheet.

3 Bake the almond pears in a preheated oven, 150°C/300°F, for about 20 minutes or until lightly coloured. Set aside to cool.

4 When the almond pears are cold, brush lightly with orange flower water or rosewater and then dust with sifted icing sugar.

oranges in caramel sauce

ingredients

SERVES 6

9 oranges

175 ml/6 fl oz water

250 g/9 oz white granulated
sugar

3 tbsp Greek honey

method

1 Using a zester, remove the zest from the oranges and put in a small saucepan. Add the water and soak for 1 hour.

2 When the orange zest has soaked, simmer for 20 minutes. Strain any remaining liquid, reserving the zest, into a measuring cup and add water to make 175 ml/ 6 fl oz.

3 Using a sharp knife, remove the peel from the oranges, discarding all the white pith. Cut the flesh widthways into 1/2-cm/1/4-inch slices and arrange in a glass serving dish, scattered with a little of the orange zest. Reserve most of the zest to decorate.

4 Put the measured water and the sugar in a saucepan and heat until the sugar has dissolved, then bring to the boil and boil rapidly until it turns a pale golden colour. Immediately remove from the heat, stir in the honey until dissolved. Cool slightly, then pour the caramel sauce over the oranges. Chill in the refrigerator for at least 3 hours before serving, decorated with the reserved zest.